Gautam

Breathe to Rise

Meenaa

Copyright © <2025> <Meenaa>

Made with ❤ on the Notion Press Platform

www.notionpress.com

To all my spiritual mentors, yoga teachers, dance coaches, physical trainers, occult science mentors, and my music therapy coach. This book is a reflection of every breath of wisdom, discipline, and inspiration that you have shared with me.

Each of you, in your own way, has taught me how to move with awareness, breathe with intention, and live with presence. From the stillness of meditation to the rhythm of dance, from the depth of breathwork to the power of energy healing—you have all shaped my journey.

This book is not just mine—it carries the essence of your teachings, your guidance, and the wisdom you have so generously shared.

With deep gratitude, respect, and breath-filled appreciation,

This book is for you.

Last but not least my son Pranav, who helps me with each and every book of mine.

Contents

Acknowledgments

Writing this book has been an extraordinary journey—one that goes beyond words and into the very breath of existence. This is not just a book about breathwork; it is a reflection of life, presence, and the silent power that moves through all of us.

First and foremost, my deepest gratitude to Gautam Patel, whose wisdom, experiences, and unwavering passion for breathwork have shaped the heart of this book. Your journey, your insights, and your dedication to sharing the transformative power of breath have made this book possible.

A heartfelt thank you to everyone who has been a part of this process.

To the mentors, teachers, and guides who have influenced Gautam's path and shared their wisdom over the years.

To the students, practitioners, and seekers who continue to explore the infinite potential of breath, reminding us that growth is a lifelong process.

To family and friends for their patience, support, and belief in this work. Your encouragement has been the silent force behind every word written here.

To the ancient wisdom traditions, modern scientific researchers, and breathwork pioneers whose contributions have deepened our understanding of this profound practice.

Special thanks to the readers—you, who are holding this book in your hands, breathing as you read. Your curiosity, openness, and willingness to explore your own breath make this book more than just pages; it becomes a living experience.

Finally, my gratitude extends to the breath itself—the quiet, ever-present force that gives us life, teaches us patience, and reminds us that everything we seek is already within.

This book is for all those who wish to breathe better, live better, and experience life fully. May every inhale bring awareness, and every exhale bring freedom.

With gratitude, Meenaa.

Introduction

The moment I knew this book had to be written.

It all started with a simple conversation. Or rather, a simple observation.

I had been speaking to Gautam Patel for a while—about life, about breathwork, about the things most people never stop to think about. And every time we talked, I noticed something strange.

He wasn't just talking about breath—he was breathing it.

His words flowed effortlessly, like a steady inhale and exhale.

His presence felt calm, grounded, unshaken—no matter the situation.

Even in the middle of deep discussions, he had this unusual ability to pause, breathe, and respond with clarity—never with rush, never with hesitation.

I thought to myself, "There's something different about the way this man breathes—and I need to understand it."

The Realization: People Are Ignoring Their Greatest Power

As our conversations deepened, I started noticing something even more profound—most people have no idea how much power is hidden in their own breath.

Think about it.

People spend years searching for ways to reduce stress, while the answer is literally inside them, waiting to be used.

People overthink every decision, while conscious breathing can bring instant clarity.

People feel overwhelmed by emotions, while a simple shift in breath can change their entire state of mind.

And yet, no one teaches us this.

We learn how to speak, but not how to breathe while speaking.

We learn how to think, but not how to breathe through uncertainty.

We learn how to run, work, argue, succeed, but never how to breathe properly while doing it all.

I realized something shocking—we live our entire lives breathing, but we never truly learn how to breathe.

That's when I knew: this book needed to exist.

Why Write This Book?

This isn't just a book about breathwork techniques. It's a book about how breath is woven into every aspect of life.

It's about how Gautam discovered breathwork—not in a monastery, but in the middle of real struggles, fears, and challenges.

It's about how breath can transform the way we handle stress, emotions, and even relationships.

It's about how something as simple as breathing can unlock deeper intuition, better health, and even stronger presence in daily life.

But more than anything—it's about remembering that breath is the one thing that has been with us since birth and will stay with us until our last moment.

And if we can master it, we can master how we experience life itself.

One Breath at a Time…

So here we are.

A book that isn't just meant to be read, but to be experienced. A book that isn't about fixing you, but about awakening what's already within you.

And all it takes is one conscious breath at a time.

Intro

Q: Gautam, how would you like to introduce yourself to your readers?

A: I am a 48-year-old man from Bharuch, Gujarat—a land where the rivers flow with stories, traditions, and resilience. My journey, like any life truly lived, has been a confluence of roles, responsibilities, and revelations.

If I had to define myself, I would say I am a seeker—of breath, of balance, of meaning. In the eyes of the world, I am a businessman, an entrepreneur who has navigated the highs and lows of commerce, understanding that success isn't just about numbers, but about the energy we bring into our work. I am a marathon runner, not just in the literal sense, but in spirit—constantly testing my endurance, both physically and mentally. And I am a breathwork practitioner, breathopreneur, someone who has found the profound connection between the simple act of breathing and the vast, intricate workings of life itself.

But if you strip away the labels, I am also a father, trying to teach my son the art of patience and resilience, and the importance of pausing to breathe when life gets overwhelming. I am a husband, understanding that love is not about grand gestures but the everyday presence we offer one another. I am a son, carrying the weight and wisdom of my ancestors while paving my own path forward. As a friend, I strive to be the kind of person who listens not just with my ears, but with my heart.

Growing up in Gujarat, I witnessed life's true wealth lies in how well we manage our inner world. Breathwork became my bridge—a way to unite ambition with mindfulness, speed with stillness, and strength with surrender.

Life, I've learned, is not segmented. The breath we take as we cross a marathon's finish line is the same breath that fuels a late-night business strategy session or a quiet moment with family. It's about finding stillness in motion, clarity in complexity, and strength in vulnerability.

I want to share these insights with you, not as prescriptions but as possibilities. We're all learning to navigate the myriad roles we play, and if my journey can offer a light, a tool, or even a moment of reflection, then I believe we're all the better for it.

I hope this book is not just about my journey but about possibilities—possibilities for you to explore, reflect, and perhaps find your own rhythm in the dance of breath and life. We are all running a marathon, in one way or another. The question is, are we running breathlessly, or are we breathing as we run?

Beginning

Q: Gautam, how did you get in the breathwork practice? And when exactly did you start?

A: If I were to say that my breath has been my greatest teacher, it wouldn't be an exaggeration. Through every phase of life—struggles, triumphs, and transitions—my breath has been the one constant. Yet, for the longest time, I never truly noticed it, never paid attention to the power it held.

Like most people, I was conditioned to believe that success meant external security—financial stability, professional achievements, social status. But deep inside, I was restless. I wanted security in life, not just in terms of material success, but on an emotional, mental, and even spiritual level. I wanted to be free from the constant fear that lived inside me.

I had a difficult childhood. Emotionally, I never felt strong enough. There were moments when I would feel an unexplainable heaviness, a sadness that I couldn't fully understand. Some situations in my family triggered emotions I didn't know how to process, and there were times when I felt deeply depressed and disconnected. I wanted to escape, but escape wasn't the solution—I needed to find a way to face those emotions, to go through them instead of running from them.

To deal with this, I turned to literature—old and new, scientific and spiritual, ancient scriptures and modern psychology. I was searching for something, anything, that could give me a sense of control over my mind and emotions. I read about meditation, philosophy, the workings of the subconscious mind, and the human nervous system. And every path, every school of thought, kept pointing me back to one fundamental force—the breath.

My training for long-distance running pushes my body beyond its limits and practicing breath work during training or even during real race, helped me to observe myself anytime, in any situation through breath.

At first, I ignored it. But over time, I noticed that experienced athletes seemed to move with an effortless rhythm, as if their breath and body were in perfect sync. I realized that breath wasn't just about survival—it was about performance, energy, and resilience.

But my real transformation began twenty years ago, when I experienced Osho's Dynamic Meditation for the first time. That first experiment changed something inside me. It wasn't just about sitting still and focusing on the breath—it was raw, intense, powerful. It used breath to break patterns, to release trapped emotions, to clear the mind of years of conditioning.

For the first time, I felt what it was like to breathe fully, deeply, consciously. I felt my body come alive in a way I had never experienced before. My mind, which was always overthinking, suddenly became clear. The fear, the emotional weight, the mental noise—it all began to dissolve.

That experience left me with an unshakable truth—breath was the bridge between my chaos and my calm.

From that moment, I immersed myself in learning. I studied breathwork intensely—reading ancient texts, modern scientific papers, whatever related literature I could get, I explored and am still exploring everything from pranayama to contemporary breath techniques. And, along this journey, my guru, Baba Purnanand Bharati, whom we lovingly call Baba, helped me a lot.

Baba isn't just a saint—he is a mirror. He didn't give me answers in prayers; he helped me find my own. I realised that breath is not just air—it is energy, consciousness, and life itself. Our every emotion, every state of mind, every pattern in life is tied to how we breathe.

With Baba's blessings and my own relentless practice, I didn't just 'learn' breathwork—I became it.

Over the past 20 years, breathwork has become my foundation. It has transformed not just my meditation practice, but my entire life—my relationships, my work, my endurance, my ability to remain calm in any situation. Through years of experimentation, I developed my own breathwork system, one that is practical, accessible, and deeply transformative.

Now, breathwork is not just something I do—it is my way of being.

Because breath is not just a tool for survival. It is a tool for mastery. Master your breath, and you master your energy. Master your energy, and you master your life.

Challenges

Q : Please share challenges you had to bear during your journey of breath work.

A : When you take a breath, have you ever thought that this breath is the greatest miracle of your life? Probably not. Because we take breathing for granted, never truly understanding its depth. But for me, this very breath was my biggest struggle—and also my greatest solution.

You asked me about the challenges I faced—both from within and from the outside. This question may seem simple, but it runs deep. I'll break it into two parts: inner struggles and external struggles. And I'll explain it not in complex terms, but in the way I have lived it—so that anyone can understand and relate to it.

The Biggest Battle Was Within.

My journey was never easy. In fact, if I'm honest, it was quite challenging. When I first started understanding 'breath,' I thought it was just about inhaling oxygen and exhaling carbon dioxide.

But as I delved deeper, I realized that breath controls our mind, emotions, energy, and even our entire existence.

In the beginning, my own breath felt heavy. When I started breathwork, I was in a strange state—my mind was restless, but my breath was stuck. Many times, I felt like my own body was my biggest obstacle.

My body reacted strangely—sometimes with discomfort, sometimes with anxiety, sometimes by bringing up old, forgotten memories. I couldn't understand what was happening. That's when I realized that our body is not just a structure of flesh and bones. It is a museum of all our memories, emotions, and past experiences. And when you dive deep into your breath, this museum opens its doors.

It was exactly like diving into a deep ocean—where, at first, everything is dark and overwhelming, but as you start swimming, you begin to experience its peace and beauty.

"I Was Confronting Myself"

The hardest part of my inner struggle was facing my subconscious mind. The fears, insecurities, and suppressed emotions within me started surfacing one by one. As I practiced deep breathing, old wounds, forgotten pains, and unprocessed feelings began to emerge.

It wasn't easy for me. But then I asked myself a simple question:

"Will I really be afraid of my own breath?"

And that's where my biggest transformation began.

External Struggles are, when the World Doesn't Understand.

If my inner battle was with my soul, my external battle was with the world. "Convincing People Was the Hardest Part"

When I started this journey, many people told me:

"Gautam, you can have a successful career, then why waste time on breathing?" Some laughed at me, some thought it was pointless.

"Come on, breathwork and meditation are fine, but they won't feed you!" Convincing people that breath is not just air but the very energy of life—that was the most difficult challenge. And this wasn't just in our country; this was the case all over the world.

Even today, when I walk into a workshop and say,

"Understand your breath, and you will understand your life,"

people first laugh, then think, and finally, when they experience it, they cry. Cry of ecstasy, cry of release, cry of suppressed emotions, cry of wasted time in life.

"The Conflict Between Science and Spirituality"

Another struggle was bringing breathwork into the space between science and spirituality. Many saw it as purely spiritual, while in reality, it is deeply scientific.

Look at NASA—they are researching 'Slow Breathing' and 'Cyclic Sighing.' Harvard and Stanford studies now confirm that the right breathing techniques can reduce stress, anxiety, and even improve brain function.

But when I first started talking about this, people saw it only as some mystical, yoga-related concept. It took me years to present it in a scientific language that people could accept.

The Biggest Lesson is: My Breath Is My Guru

Now, when I look back, I see that all these struggles became my greatest teachers. When I sat with my breath, I met my fears.

When I slowed my breath, my anxiety disappeared.

When I deepened my breath, I felt myself open up. And when I took my first "victorious breath," I knew I was truly free. Today, this is exactly what I teach my students:

"If you learn to control your breath, you learn to control your life."

This is not just a theory—it is life-changing.

My Message to my readers is, the more struggles you face inside, the deeper your breath should be. If you feel stuck in life—stress, anxiety, fear, insecurity—just focus on your breath.

Slowly…

Breathe deeply…

Feel every inhale and exhale…

And watch how your life starts changing.

Because the solution to every problem in life is hidden in your next breath. Just take one deep breath… and see!

Reactions of Close Ones

Q : How did Your close ones react to these practices?

A : Transformation is not just about changing yourself; it's about navigating the reactions of those around you. When you begin walking a new path—especially one that challenges conventional wisdom—you inevitably meet resistance, skepticism, and sometimes silent observation.

In my case, my close family neither encouraged me nor discouraged me. They stood at a neutral ground—not actively pushing me toward breathwork, but not pulling me away from it either. At the time, I didn't realize how important that neutrality was. Looking back, I see that their silence gave me the space I needed to explore, experiment, and ultimately transform.

But not everyone in my life responded in the same way. Some found my journey inspiring, some found it amusing, and others found it unsettling.

Let me take you through the reactions I encountered.

My family has always been practical. They believed in working hard, earning a living, and staying grounded in reality.

"That sigh is breathwork, just untrained. What if I told you that you could control it, amplify it, and use it to change the way you feel?"

I told this to one of my close friends. He took the challenge. Attended my personal sessions. Then what he experienced was just phenomenal.

My father was the same. He never told me to stop, never dismissed it outright. He didn't actively participate in my journey, but he didn't create obstacles either. That neutrality, I later realized, was a form of quiet support. They were waiting to see what would come of it. Friends are different from family—they don't hesitate to speak their minds. And when you do something unconventional, they really don't hold back.

"Gautam, have you turned into a sage now?"

"Are you going to start living in a cave?"

"Why are you breathing like a dragon?"

At first, it was all jokes. They found it hilarious that I was taking something as 'simple' as breathing so seriously.

But something fascinating happened over time.

One by one, the same friends who mocked me started approaching me in private.

"Bro, I've been having trouble sleeping. Can you teach me that thing you do?" "I get anxious before meetings. Will this breathwork stuff actually help?"

"I tried holding my breath for two minutes after watching a documentary. I almost fainted. Am I doing it wrong?"

It was incredible to watch the shift. The same people who laughed at me were now asking me for help. It taught me something valuable: people resist what they don't understand, but they listen when they see results.

One of my closest friends, who had severe performance anxiety, tried coherent breathing (a simple method of breathing at a steady rhythm of five seconds in, five seconds out) for two weeks before his next big presentation.

After the event, he called me and said,

"Gautam, I don't know what you did to me, but for the first time in years, I wasn't nervous. This stuff actually works!"

But not all reactions were positive. Some were deeply uncomfortable with my transformation.

I remember someone close to me saying,

"You're different now. You don't react the way you used to."

It wasn't a compliment—it was a concern.

For them, my change was unsettling. I wasn't engaging in pointless arguments, I wasn't complaining about stress, I wasn't reacting emotionally to situations that would have triggered me before. And that made them uncomfortable.

"Do you even care anymore?" someone once asked me.

The truth was, I cared more than ever. But I had stopped reacting in the way they were used to. Instead of being consumed by stress, I had learned to breathe through it.

Instead of being hijacked by emotions, I had learned to witness them.

Not everyone liked that change. Some people missed the old, submissive me—the one who would get riled up, who would engage in the drama of everyday life. But I wasn't that person anymore.

And that's one of the hardest parts of personal transformation: it doesn't just change you; it changes your relationships.

Over time, things changed. The more people saw me evolve, the more they started believing. Some of my skeptical friends introduced their own families to breathwork. The people who once found my transformation unsettling eventually found comfort in it.

It's not about convincing people—it's about embodying the change until they see the results for themselves.

change is uncomfortable, both for you and for those around you. When you do something unconventional—whether it's breathwork, mindfulness, or any deep inner work—people won't always understand.

At first, they will resist.

Then, they will question.

Then, they will joke.

Then, they will observe.

And finally… they will follow.

If you're on a similar journey, remember this: you don't need people's approval to grow. Just keep going. Keep breathing. Keep evolving. One day, the same people who doubted you will ask you for guidance.

And that is the real power of breath.

Physical Benefits

Q : Please explain Physical Benefits of Breathwork.

A : If I asked you, "What's the most important thing in your life?" you might say your family, career, health, or passions. But the truth is, without your breath, none of those things would exist.

Breath is the foundation of everything—yet most people don't think about it until they're gasping for air.

Now, let's talk about what happens when you start paying attention to your breath—how it transforms your body, energy, and physical health in ways you never imagined.

1. Oxygenation: More Oxygen, More Energy

Most of us breathe too fast, too shallow, and too unconsciously. This means we're not using our lungs properly, and our body isn't getting the full oxygen supply it needs. When you do proper breathwork:

Your lungs expand more.

More oxygen reaches your blood.

Your body produces more ATP (energy molecules) at a cellular level. More stamina (for workouts, sports, and daily life).

Less fatigue (because your cells are getting what they need).

Faster recovery after physical exertion.

Think of your breath like the fuel supply of a car. The deeper and more efficiently you breathe, the better your "engine" runs.

2. Nervous System Balance: From Stress to Relaxation

Your nervous system has two major states:

Fight-or-flight mode (sympathetic nervous system – stress, anxiety, high alert). Rest-and-digest mode (parasympathetic nervous system – relaxation, recovery, healing).

Most of us are stuck in a permanent fight-or-flight state due to work stress, personal responsibilities, and modern life. This constant tension leads to:

Increased heart rate.

Shallow breathing.

High blood pressure.

Poor digestion.

Weakened immune system.

Breathwork activates your parasympathetic nervous system, meaning:

Your heart rate slows down.

Your blood pressure drops.

Your body moves into a state of healing and recovery.

One of the simplest techniques is, Slow breathing (5-6 breaths per minute) instantly shifts your nervous system from stress to calm.

3. Improved Lung Capacity and Strength

Most people only use 30-40% of their lung capacity.

When you train your breath, you expand your lungs fully, making them stronger and more efficient.

Breathwork helps:

Increase lung function (use more of your lungs).

Strengthen respiratory muscles (diaphragm, intercostal muscles).

Clear excess CO_2 build-up (which often causes brain fog and fatigue).

Studies show that deep diaphragmatic breathing can increase lung capacity by up to 30% over time.

That's why athletes, free divers, and yogis train their breath—it directly enhances physical endurance.

4. Cardiovascular Health: Better Blood Circulation and Lower Blood Pressure

When you breathe deeply and correctly:

Your blood vessels expand (better circulation).

Your heart doesn't have to work as hard (lower heart rate).

Your blood pressure stabilizes.

A simple 4-7-8 breathing technique (inhale for 4, hold for 7, exhale for 8) has been proven to: Lower blood pressure naturally.

Reduce the risk of heart disease.

Improve overall cardiovascular efficiency.

Breath is not just air—it's your heart's rhythm regulator.

5. Detoxification: Cleansing the Body

Did you know that 70% of the body's toxins are expelled through breathing?

When you exhale, you're not just releasing carbon dioxide—you're also removing waste from your cells.

Shallow breathers retain more toxins in their body, leading to:

Fatigue, Brain fog, Weakened immunity, Anxiety.

Deep, conscious breathwork helps:

Improve lymphatic drainage (natural detox process).

Support kidney and liver function (filtering waste).

Enhance cellular regeneration (renewing your body from within).

A simple full-lung breathing exercise (expanding belly, ribs, and chest fully) flushes out stagnant air, helping your body function at peak efficiency.

6. Enhanced Physical Endurance and Stamina

If you've ever run out of breath during a workout, you know how important breath control is for endurance.

Breathwork techniques like "hypoxic training" (holding your breath for short intervals) improve: Oxygen efficiency in muscles.

Endurance for sports, running, and exercise,

the body's ability to perform under pressure.

That's why top athletes—from marathon runners to MMA fighters—train their breath before they train their body.

The rule is simple:

The better your breath control, the longer you can push yourself physically.

7. Strengthened Immunity and Faster Recovery

When you breathe deeply, your:

White blood cell production increases (stronger immune system).

Inflammation levels drop (reducing chronic pain).

Cells regenerate faster (wounds heal quicker).

Breathwork has been shown to boost immune function, helping the body fight off infections naturally.

One famous study on Wim Hof (The Iceman) showed that through breath training, he was able to:

Control his immune response.

Resist extreme cold.

Reduce inflammation in his body.

If your immune system is strong, your body doesn't get sick as easily—and breathwork is one of the simplest ways to strengthen it.

8. Better Sleep and Reduced Snoring

Poor breathing habits (especially mouth breathing) contribute to:

Sleep apnea, Snoring,

Insomnia.

Breathwork before bed helps:

Activate melatonin production (sleep hormone).

Shift the nervous system to deep relaxation mode.

Open up airways, reducing snoring and apnea symptoms.

A simple "box breathing" (inhale 4, hold 4, exhale 4, hold 4) before bed can dramatically improve sleep quality. Breathwork Is a Superpower.

Most people go through life without ever using their breath to its full potential. They breathe too fast, too shallow, and without awareness. And as a result, they experience fatigue, stress, and poor health.

But when you learn to breathe consciously and correctly, you unlock:

More energy,

More focus.

A stronger body.

A healthier heart.

A longer life.

If food is fuel for your body, then breath is the spark that ignites it.

Change your breath, and you change your life.

Change In Mental State

Q : How Breathwork Can Change a Person's Mental State?

A : Imagine a stormy ocean. The waves are crashing, the wind is howling, and everything feels chaotic. Now imagine a deep, still lake—calm, clear, and peaceful.

Your mind works the same way. Most people live in the storm—restless, anxious, overthinking, constantly reacting to everything around them. But what if I told you that your breath is the key to shifting from the storm to the still lake?

Breathwork is not just about improving physical health—it is one of the most powerful tools to regulate emotions, calm the mind, and transform your mental state.

Let me break it down for you.

1. Your Breath Controls Your Nervous System

Your mind and emotions are deeply connected to your nervous system, which has two main states:

a. Fight-or-Flight Mode (Sympathetic Nervous System) → Stress & Anxiety

Heart rate increases.

Breathing becomes shallow and fast.

Mind races with thoughts and worries.

Body tenses up, preparing for "danger" (even if the danger is just an email or traffic jam). b. Rest-and-Digest Mode (Parasympathetic Nervous System) → Calm & Clarity

Heart rate slows down.

Breathing becomes deep and rhythmic.

Mind becomes clear and focused.

Body relaxes and starts healing.

Most people are stuck in fight-or-flight mode all the time, which leads to chronic stress, anxiety, and emotional instability.

Breathwork is the fastest way to shift from stress to calm—by directly activating your parasympathetic nervous system.

Try this right now:

Inhale slowly through your nose for 4 seconds.

Hold your breath for 4 seconds.

Exhale slowly for 8 seconds.

Repeat 5 times.

Feel the difference? Your mind slows down instantly.

2. Breath and Anxiety: Stopping the "Mental Overload"

Anxiety feels like your brain is stuck in overdrive—thoughts keep racing, you feel restless, and your body is tense.

Breathing is the "off switch" for anxiety.

When you slow down your breath, you:

Reduce the production of stress hormones (cortisol & adrenaline).

Increase oxygen supply to the brain, improving clarity.

Send a signal to the brain: "You are safe. Relax."

Best Breathing Technique for Anxiety: "Coherent Breathing"

Inhale for 5 seconds.

Exhale for 5 seconds.

Repeat for 5 minutes.

This simple technique synchronizes your heart rate and brain waves, creating a deep sense of calm.

3. Breathwork and Depression: Awakening the Mind

Depression often feels like a heavy fog in the mind—low energy, lack of motivation, emotional numbness.

When someone is depressed, their breath becomes shallow and slow, which lowers oxygen levels in the body and brain. This makes the person feel even more sluggish. Breathwork is like an internal wake-up call. It increases oxygen flow, boosts energy, and releases feel-good neurotransmitters like serotonin and dopamine.

Best Breathing Technique for Low Mood: "Bellows Breath (Bhastrika)"

Inhale deeply and quickly through the nose.

Exhale forcefully through the nose.

Repeat for 30 seconds.

Warning: This is an energizing technique—use it when you need a mental boost, not before sleep! And always better to do under professional guidance.

Within 60 seconds, you will feel an immediate shift in energy and mental clarity.

4. Emotional Regulation: Controlling Anger, Fear, and Sadness

Your breath mirrors your emotions.

Angry? Your breath is fast and shallow.

Fearful? Your breath is irregular.

Sad? Your breath is slow and heavy.

What if I told you that by changing your breath, you can change the way you feel?

Your emotions follow your breath—not the other way around.

Next time you feel anger, sadness, or fear, instead of reacting, focus on your breath. Best Breathing Technique for Emotional Stability: "Box Breathing"

This technique is used by Navy SEALs to stay calm under extreme pressure. It teaches your brain that you are in control of your emotions—not the other way around.

5. Mental Clarity & Focus: Breath is Brain Power

Ever feel mentally foggy, distracted, or unable to concentrate?

That's because your brain is not getting enough oxygen.

Breathwork can:

Increase oxygen supply to the brain, improving focus.

Enhance brainwave synchronization, creating mental sharpness.

Reduce mental fatigue, making you feel more alert.

Best Breathing Technique for Focus: "Alternate Nostril Breathing (Nadi Shodhana)"

Close your right nostril, inhale through the left.

Close your left nostril, exhale through the right.

Inhale through the right, exhale through the left.

Repeat for 5 minutes.

This balances both hemispheres of the brain, improving focus, decision-making, and cognitive function.

6. Healing Trauma: Releasing Stored Pain

Your body holds onto past trauma—especially in your breath.

When you experience something painful, your breath becomes restricted. Many people unknowingly carry old pain in their breathing patterns.

Deep breathwork practices—like Rebirthing Breathwork or Holotropic Breathing—help release:-

Suppressed emotions.

Unprocessed grief or trauma.

Energy blocks in the body.

Many people cry during deep breathwork. Not because they are sad, but because they are releasing what they've held onto for years.

7. Creativity and Intuition: Accessing Higher States

Did you know that breathwork can enhance creativity?

It activates the right hemisphere of the brain, linked to imagination.

It opens up the pineal gland, associated with intuition.

It creates a flow state—where ideas and inspiration come naturally.

Many artists, musicians, and thinkers use breath techniques before creating their best work. Best Breathing Technique for Creativity: "Deep Diaphragmatic Breathing"

Inhale deeply, expanding the belly.

Hold for 5 seconds.

Exhale slowly.

Repeat until your mind feels open.

Breathwork is a Mental Reset Button.

Your breath is the only function in your body that is both automatic and controllable.

When you control your breath, you control:

Your emotions.

Your thoughts.

Your state of mind.

If you change the way you breathe, you will change the way you live.

Next time you feel stressed, anxious, or overwhelmed…

Instead of reacting, pause.

Take a deep breath.

Then another.

Then one more.

Because the power to shift your mind is always right under your nose.

Spiritual Benefits

Q : Any spiritual uplifting?

A : If someone had asked me years ago whether breathwork could lead to spiritual growth, I might have shrugged. Like many people, I assumed that spirituality was something separate—something for monks, sages, or those who renounced the world.

But the deeper I went into my breath, the more I realized: spirituality is not about escaping life; it's about fully living it. And breath is the bridge.

Let me take you through how breathwork can awaken consciousness, deepen spiritual connection, and transform your perception of life itself.

1. Breath is a Gateway to Higher Consciousness.

Every spiritual tradition—whether it's yoga, Zen, Sufism, Taoism, or indigenous shamanic practices—has used breath as a tool for awakening. Why? Because breath is the direct link between body, mind, and spirit.

Here's the simplest truth:

When your breath is shallow, your awareness is limited.

When your breath is deep and conscious, your awareness expands.

When you breathe fully, something shifts inside you:

Your mind quiets.

Your ego softens.

You become present—fully alive in the moment.

In those moments, you don't "think" about spirituality— you feel it.

2. The Power of the Present Moment: Breath as Meditation

Most people struggle with meditation because their minds are too restless. "I can't stop thinking."

"I get distracted."

"I don't know if I'm doing it right."

But here's the secret: breathing itself is meditation.

Every inhale brings life force (prana, chi, energy) into you.

Every exhale releases tension, old patterns, negativity.

When you focus on your breath, you automatically enter a meditative state—without forcing it.

Try this now:

Inhale deeply for 5 seconds.

Hold for 5 seconds.

Exhale completely for 10 seconds.

Repeat 5 times.

Notice the shift? Your mind slows down, and you become more aware of this moment.

That awareness—pure presence—is the foundation of spiritual awakening.

3. Breathwork and Expanded States of Consciousness

Certain breath techniques can take you into altered states of consciousness—similar to deep meditation, psychedelic experiences, or profound moments of insight.

One of the most powerful methods is Holotropic Breathing (developed by Dr. Stanislav Grof), which involves:

Deep, continuous breathing (without pausing between inhales & exhales). Rhythmic intensity that increases oxygen levels in the brain.

A shift in brain waves—moving from beta (thinking) to theta (intuitive, dream-like state).

People who practice intensive breathwork sessions report:

Feeling one with the universe.

Receiving deep insights about their purpose.

Releasing old emotional blockages.

Experiencing visions, memories, or even past-life recall.

The reason? Breath has the power to unlock hidden layers of consciousness. It is like opening a door inside yourself—one that you didn't even know existed. 4. Use breath as a Mirror.

The biggest obstacle to spiritual growth is the ego—the false sense of self that keeps us trapped in:

Overthinking,

Attachments,

Fears,

Self-doubt.

When you control the breath, you weaken the ego.

Here's why:

The ego feeds on mental noise—but deep breathing silences the mind.

The ego clings to identities—but breath reminds you that you are more than just a name, job, or role.

The ego resists surrender—but breath teaches you to let go.

During breathwork, there are moments where you feel completely free—where there is no "me" and "you," no past and future—just pure existence.

That feeling? That is your true self. That is spirituality.

4. Feeling One with Everything

In the Bhagavad Gita, Upanishads, Tao Te Ching, and Sufi poetry, there is a recurring theme: "The breath is the divine within you."

If you go deep enough into your breath, you start realizing something profound:

The same air that moves through you is moving through every living being. The trees, the animals, the oceans—they all breathe, just like you.

There is no separation—only connection.

Many spiritual seekers spend years searching for enlightenment, but the secret is right under their nose—literally.

When you breathe with full awareness, you realize:

You are not just a drop in the ocean. You are the ocean in a drop.

5. Breathwork Transforms Daily Life Spiritually

Spirituality is not about escaping the world. It's about transforming how you live within it.

When you practice breathwork regularly, your daily life changes in ways that feel almost miraculous:

You react less, observe more.

You stop worrying about the future, because you trust life.

You become more grateful for simple things—like the air filling your lungs. You feel a deep inner peace, no matter what's happening around you.

You don't have to chant mantras, follow rituals, or sit in meditation for hours. Just breathe deeply, with full awareness.

That is meditation.

That is prayer.

That is connection to the divine.

Your Breath is Your Guru.

Many people search for teachers, books, and external guidance to grow spiritually. But the greatest teacher is already within you. Your breath.

Every inhale is an invitation to wake up.

Every exhale is an invitation to let go.

If you want to experience something beyond the mind—breathe consciously. If you want to break free from mental chatter—breathe deeply.

If you want to feel connected to something greater—breathe with awareness.

Because in the end, breath is not just life.

Breath is wisdom. Breath is liberation. Breath is YOU.

Support of Close Ones

Q : If people around us, family, friends or close ones, don't support us or make fun of our practice, then what do you suggest ? How should one go about it?

A : "What to Do When People Around You Don't Support or Mock Your Practice" Let's be honest—when you walk an unconventional path, not everyone will understand it.

You might start a new practice—whether it's breathwork, meditation, yoga, or any kind of self-improvement—and suddenly, you realize:

Your family doesn't take it seriously.

Your friends make jokes about it.

Your close ones think you're wasting time.

And it stings. Because deep down, we all want validation. We all want the people we love to at least respect our choices, if not support them.

So what do you do when that validation doesn't come?

Do you quit?

Do you argue?

Do you try to convince them?

Here's my take—don't waste your energy fighting for approval.

Instead, focus on your practice. Be your own proof.

**1. Understand That Their Reactions Are Not About
You**

First, let's get one thing straight:

When people mock or dismiss your practice, it's not about
you—it's about them.

Most of the time, people react negatively because of:

Lack of understanding – They don't know how powerful
breathwork (or any inner work) can be. Fear of change –
They are uncomfortable seeing you evolve, especially if
they are stuck in their own patterns.

Conditioning – Society has trained people to only respect
things that have a "tangible" outcome (like money, status,
or job titles).

Ego resistance – If you become calmer, stronger, and
more self-aware, it may make them question their own
way of living.

When someone says, "Oh, you're into all this spiritual
stuff now?" or "Why waste time breathing when you do
it naturally?"—what they're actually saying is,

"I don't understand this, so I'm going to make fun of it."

Your job is NOT to make them understand. Your job is to
keep going.

**2. Stop Expecting Support and Start Supporting
Yourself**

One of the biggest reasons people quit their practice is because they expect support from those around them.

"If my family believed in me, I'd be more motivated."

"If my friends respected my practice, I'd feel more confident."

But let me ask you:

Did you start breathwork for THEM, or for YOU?

Because if it's truly for you, then why does their approval matter?

Here's a hard but powerful truth:

If you need outside validation to continue, your practice is weak.

If you are committed even without support, your practice is unbreakable.

3. Lead by Example, Not by Argument.

I've seen many people get into heated debates with their family or friends, trying to explain: "No, breathwork is real science!"

"This can change your nervous system!"

"Look at all these research studies!"

But here's the thing—

People don't believe words. They believe the results.

Instead of arguing, be the proof.

Let them see the transformation in you:

Your calmness under stress.

Your increased energy.

Your clarity in decision-making.

Your better health.

When they notice you're not reacting like before…

When they see you're handling challenges better…

When they realize you're happier, lighter, and more balanced…

They'll start getting curious. And when curiosity replaces resistance, they will come to you. 4. Set Boundaries with Negativity.

Not everyone will support you, and that's okay. But some people will actively try to pull you down.

They'll mock you.

They'll discourage you.

They'll make you feel like an outsider.

If that happens, ask yourself:

"Do I need this energy in my life?"

Because here's the reality—you don't have to tolerate negativity, even if it comes from family or close friends.

Setting boundaries doesn't mean cutting people off; it means choosing what energy you allow into your space.

If someone constantly dismisses your practice, stop discussing it with them. If a friend always mocks you, spend less time with them.

If your family doesn't respect it, practice quietly without needing their validation. Protect your peace. Protect your path.

4. Find Like-Minded People.

One of the easiest ways to stay committed when your close ones don't support you is to surround yourself with people who do.

Join a breathwork or meditation community.

Find online groups or forums where people share their experiences.

Attend workshops where you can meet people on the same path.

This is important because we are social beings—we need to feel understood and connected. And if you don't get that from your immediate circle, find your soul family elsewhere. A supportive community will remind you that you are not alone in this journey.

5. Remember, your Journey Is Your Own.

At the end of the day, your breath is your breath.

Your mind is your mind.

Your peace is your peace.

No one can breathe for you.

No one can meditate for you.

No one can do the inner work for you.

So why should their opinion stop you?

Some of the greatest minds in history—whether it's Buddha, Socrates, or even modern thinkers like Steve Jobs—all walked their paths despite resistance.

Every great transformation starts with a person who is willing to be different. Keep Going, No Matter What. If your family, friends, or society doesn't support you, don't take it personally. They are simply operating from their own level of awareness. Your job is not to convince them. Your job is to keep growing. Your transformation will speak louder than your words ever could.

So the next time someone mocks your practice or doesn't take it seriously, just smile and breathe. Because while they are wasting their breath on doubt,

you are using yours to evolve.

Ketan Desai

My brother, Ketan Desai, has been a constant source of inspiration in my journey. Our shared passion for sports, especially tennis and marathons, has strengthened our bond over the years. Training together pushes me to stay disciplined, and his commitment to fitness motivates me to go beyond my limits.

What I admire most about him is his dedication and mindset. Whether it's waking up early for a long run or strategizing for a tennis match, his focus and perseverance set a high standard. Traveling together for marathons in different states and countries has been an incredible experience—not just for the sport, but for the lessons we learn along the way about resilience, adaptability, and teamwork.

Beyond athletics, he has always supported my journey as a Breathopreneur. He understands the power of breathwork and mindfulness, often engaging in deep discussions with me about their impact on performance and well-being. His encouragement keeps me motivated, and I am grateful to have a brother who not only shares my passions but also challenges me to grow every day.

Beginners

Q : And how much time do you think should be given to it as a beginner?

A : "How Much Time Should a Beginner Dedicate to Breathwork?" One of the most common questions I get is: "Gautam, how much time should I spend on breathwork?"

And my answer is always the same:

Start small, but be consistent.

You don't need to meditate for hours like a monk. You don't need to completely change your lifestyle overnight. But you do need to commit to showing up every day, even if it's just for a few minutes.

Let me break it down for you.

1. The 5-Minute Rule for Absolute Beginners:

If you're completely new to breathwork, start with just 5 minutes a day.

That's it.

5 minutes in the morning → To set the tone for the day.

5 minutes at night → To release stress and prepare for sleep.

That's just 10 minutes daily, but the benefits are massive:

Calmer mind.

Increased focus.

Lower stress levels.

More energy.

If you can't find 5 minutes, ask yourself:

"Am I really that busy, or am I just not prioritizing my well-being?"

You don't need more time. You just need intention.

2. Ideal Daily Routine for a Beginner is 15-20 Minutes:

Once you're comfortable with 5-minute sessions, gradually expand to 15-20 minutes a day.

Morning Practice (5-10 minutes) – Energizing & grounding

Afternoon Reset (5 minutes) – Releasing midday tension

Evening Wind-Down (5-10 minutes) – Relaxation & better sleep

Example Routine for a Beginner:

Morning (5-10 min) – Deep Diaphragmatic Breathing (for energy & focus)

Afternoon (5 min) – Coherent Breathing (to reset stress)

Night (5-10 min) – 4-7-8 Breathing (to relax & sleep better)

By committing to just 15-20 minutes a day, you will start feeling:

Less stress.

Better mood.

More clarity & emotional balance.

3. How to fit Breathwork into your day without adding more "Work":

The best part? You don't need extra time.

You can integrate breathwork into your daily activities:

While showering – Practice slow, conscious breathing.

During a commute – Try box breathing instead of mindlessly scrolling your phone. Before meals – Take 3 deep breaths to activate digestion.

Before sleep – Do 4-7-8 breathing to calm your nervous system.

Breathwork isn't something separate from life—it's something you weave into your life.

4. Advanced Practitioners can practice 30-60 Minutes a Day:

If you're serious about breathwork and want to dive deeper, then 30-60 minutes a day can take you to another level. And there will be time when you would be doing it 24/7 without much effort.

This level of practice leads to:

Profound clarity & insight.

Emotional healing & trauma release.

Deep spiritual awareness.

But don't force yourself. Build up gradually.

5. The Key is Consistency Over Duration:

The most important thing? It's better to practice for 5 minutes every day than 60 minutes once a week.

Think of it like brushing your teeth.

You don't skip brushing just because you're busy. You do it daily, even for a few minutes. Breathwork is the same. A little, every day, is better than a lot, once in a while. Because in the end, your breath is your greatest gift—why not explore it?

Before and Now

Q: Gautam, what are the top 5 differences between today's Gautam and the Gautam from 20 years ago, before breathwork became a part of your life?

A: If I look back at myself from 20 years ago, I almost feel like I'm looking at a different person. Breathwork didn't just change a few aspects of my life—it transformed everything. Here are the five biggest differences between who I was back then and who I am today:

1. From Living in Survival Mode to Living with Awareness

Then: I was constantly in survival mode—always anxious, always feeling like I was fighting against life. My mind was either stuck in the past or racing toward the future. I was restless, distracted, and caught in the endless loop of stress, self-doubt, and worry.

Now: I live in a state of awareness. I respond instead of reacting. Breathwork has given me the ability to slow down, observe my emotions without being consumed by them, and live in the present moment. I no longer feel like life is something happening to me—I feel like I am in sync with it.

2. From Emotional Instability to Emotional Mastery

Then: My emotions controlled me. Fear, anger, sadness— whenever they came, they completely overtook me. I had no real tools to process them, so I either suppressed them or let them consume me. Small triggers could ruin my entire day.

Now: I control my emotions, not the other way around. Breathwork has taught me how to release negative emotions before they take over. It's not that I don't feel fear or anger anymore—I do. But now, I know how to process them without letting them dictate my actions or decisions.

3. From Mental Chaos to Clarity and Focus

Then: My mind was a mess. I had constant overthinking, self-doubt, and negative thought loops. There were days when I felt completely lost, questioning everything in my life. Even when I was working, my mind was scattered, jumping from one thing to another.

Now: I experience deep mental clarity. I can focus fully on one thing at a time. Whether I'm making a business decision, running a marathon, or simply spending time with my family, I am fully present in what I do. Breathwork has helped me clear the unnecessary noise and access a state of deep mental stillness whenever I need it.

4. From Physical Exhaustion to High Energy and Vitality

Then: Despite being active, I often felt exhausted. I was eating well and exercising, yet something always felt off. My energy levels were unstable—I would have bursts of motivation followed by complete burnout.

Now: My energy levels are consistently high throughout the day. I don't experience the ups and downs I used to. Through breathwork, I've learned how to tap into my body's natural energy reserves, and I no longer depend on external stimulants like caffeine or motivation.

5. From Fear of Uncertainty to Trusting the Flow of Life

Then: I used to fear uncertainty. The unknown scared me. I needed to control every outcome, plan every detail, and make sure things went my way. Whenever life didn't go according to plan, I would panic or feel defeated.

Now: I have surrendered to life's flow. Breathwork has taught me that the more I try to control things, the more I suffer. Now, I trust that life unfolds exactly as it should. I don't resist change—I embrace it. I no longer let fear of the unknown hold me back.

These five changes didn't happen overnight. It took years of practice, discipline, and surrender. But today, when I look back, I know that every breath I took with awareness brought me to this point. And if I could change, anyone can.

Names

Q: Gautam, can you share the names of some breathwork techniques that you practice and teach?

A: Absolutely. Over the years, I have explored, practiced, and refined various breathwork techniques, blending ancient wisdom with modern understanding. Here are a few powerful techniques that I regularly practice and teach:

1. Dynamic Breathwork (inspired by Osho's Dynamic Meditation)

This is an intense and powerful technique that uses rapid, deep, and chaotic breathing to release stored emotions, break subconscious patterns, and awaken deep inner energy. It's one of the most transformative practices for clearing emotional baggage and resetting the nervous system.

2. Deep Rhythmic Breathing (Conscious Energy Breathing)

This technique involves slow, deep, and rhythmic breaths to oxygenate the body, calm the mind, and enter a meditative state. It helps with stress reduction, mental clarity, and emotional balance.

3. Tri-Phase Breath Technique

A three-part breathing method that includes:

1. Active breath – Quick, forceful breaths to activate energy

2. Harmonic breath – Even, balanced breathing to create inner coherence 3. Silent breath – Gentle, subtle breath to deepen awareness and connect with stillness This method helps to increase focus, release fatigue, and cultivate inner peace.

4. Box Breathing (Square Breathing)

A structured breathwork technique where you inhale, hold, exhale, and hold again for equal counts (e.g., 4-4-4-4). It's widely used for:

Calming the nervous system

Enhancing mental focus

Improving resilience under stress

5. Soma Breathwork (Rhythmic Breathing + Breath Holds)

Inspired by ancient pranayama practices, this method involves rhythmic breathing followed by breath holds to access altered states of consciousness, improve lung capacity, and boost vitality.

6. Diaphragmatic Breathing (Belly Breathing)

One of the most fundamental breathing techniques, diaphragmatic breathing engages the belly rather than the chest, allowing deeper oxygenation and relaxation. It's particularly useful for reducing anxiety, improving digestion, and enhancing respiratory health.

7. Coherent Breathing (Heart-Brain Synchronization)

A technique where you breathe at a steady rhythm of 5–6 breaths per minute to bring the heart and brain into a state of synchronization. This is highly effective for emotional balance, deep relaxation, and stress management.

8. Tummo Breathing (Inner Fire Breath)

A Tibetan technique that involves forceful breathing combined with visualization to generate inner heat and enhance endurance. It's known for boosting immune function and mental clarity.

9. Rebirthing Breathwork

A deep-connected breathing method that helps to release subconscious trauma, improve self-awareness, and heal emotional wounds.

10. Alternate Nostril Breathing (Nadi Shodhana Pranayama)

A yogic breathing technique that balances the left and right hemispheres of the brain, enhancing mental clarity, relaxation, and inner harmony.

Each of these techniques serves a unique purpose, whether it's for energy activation, emotional healing, stress reduction, or spiritual awakening. The key is to practice them with awareness, consistency, and proper guidance.

I will be glad to share additional breathwork techniques from various traditions and modern practices that I have explored and integrated into my teachings:

11. Pranayama (Yogic Breathing Techniques)

Originating from ancient Indian yoga practices, Pranayama encompasses various techniques aimed at controlling the breath to enhance the flow of prana, or life energy, within the body. Some notable Pranayama techniques include:

Ujjayi (Victorious Breath): Involves a gentle constriction at the back of the throat during inhalation and exhalation, producing a soft, oceanic sound. This technique is believed to calm the mind and increase oxygen consumption.

Kapalabhati (Skull Shining Breath): Consists of forceful exhalations followed by passive inhalations, aiming to cleanse the respiratory system and invigorate the mind.

Nadi Shodhana (Alternate Nostril Breathing): Entails alternating the breath between nostrils to balance the body's energy channels, promoting mental clarity and emotional stability.

12. Xingqi (Circulating Breath) in Traditional Chinese Medicine

Xingqi, translating to "circulating breath," is a practice in Traditional Chinese Medicine that focuses on guiding the breath through the body's meridians to balance internal energy, or qi. This technique is often integrated into qigong and tai chi practices to enhance vitality and promote healing.

13. Anapanasati (Mindfulness of Breathing) in Buddhism

Anapanasati, meaning "mindfulness of breathing," is a fundamental meditation practice in Buddhism. It involves focusing attention on the breath's natural flow to develop deep concentration and insight, leading to heightened mindfulness and inner peace.

14. Wim Hof Method

Developed by Wim Hof, this method combines specific breathing techniques with cold exposure and meditation. The breathing component involves cycles of deep inhalations followed by

passive exhalations, culminating in breath retention phases. This practice aims to influence the autonomic nervous system, enhance immune response, and improve mental well-being.

15. Holotropic Breathwork

Created by Stanislav Grof, Holotropic Breathwork employs accelerated breathing patterns paired with evocative music to induce altered states of consciousness. This technique is utilized for deep psychological exploration and emotional healing.

16. Buteyko Breathing Method

Developed by Dr. Konstantin Buteyko, this method focuses on shallow nasal breathing to increase carbon dioxide levels in the blood, aiming to improve conditions like asthma and reduce anxiety.

17. Integrative Breathing Techniques

Integrative breathing combines elements from various breathing practices to address specific therapeutic needs, such as managing stress, enhancing emotional regulation, and supporting recovery from trauma.

Each of these techniques offers unique benefits, and their effectiveness can vary based on individual needs and contexts. It's essential to approach these practices with mindfulness and, when possible, under the guidance of a qualified instructor.

Incorporating these diverse breathwork practices into my routine has profoundly impacted my physical health, mental clarity, and emotional resilience. I encourage those interested to explore these techniques, honoring their origins and adapting them to their personal journeys.

Breath Hold

Q : What do you have to say about breath holding exercise?

A : Breath-holding, or the practice of intentionally pausing respiration, has been a subject of interest across various disciplines, including sports science, medicine, and wellness. Engaging in controlled breath-holding exercises can offer several benefits, but it's essential to approach this practice with caution and awareness of potential risks under professional guidance.

Benefits of Breath-Holding are:

1. Enhanced Respiratory Efficiency:

Regular breath-holding can improve the body's tolerance to hypoxia (low oxygen levels) and hypercapnia (elevated carbon dioxide levels). This adaptation may lead to reduced breathlessness and more efficient breathing patterns during physical activities.

2. Improved Athletic Performance:

Training that includes breath-holding techniques has been shown to enhance both aerobic and anaerobic performance. Athletes may experience increased endurance and a higher threshold for fatigue.

3. Strengthened Diaphragm Function:

Holding the breath until a strong urge to inhale is felt provides a workout for the diaphragm, potentially leading to a more robust and efficient respiratory muscle.

4. Stress Reduction and Mental Clarity:

Certain breath-holding techniques can activate the parasympathetic nervous system, promoting relaxation and mental clarity. This activation may help in managing stress and enhancing focus.

5. Precautions and Risks:

Risk of Hypoxia:

Prolonged breath-holding can lead to dangerously low oxygen levels, increasing the risk of loss of consciousness or, in extreme cases, brain injury.

Cardiovascular Strain:

Breath-holding can cause significant fluctuations in blood pressure and heart rate, which may pose risks for individuals with cardiovascular conditions.

Loss of Consciousness:

Especially during activities like swimming, breath-holding can lead to shallow water blackout, a sudden loss of consciousness due to hypoxia, which can be fatal.

Research indicates that breath-holding can serve as a model to study the body's response to hypoxia and hypercapnia, providing insights into respiratory control mechanisms.

Studies on elite breath-hold divers have shown physiological adaptations that might improve both aerobic and anaerobic performance, suggesting potential benefits for athletes.

Always practice breath-holding exercises under the guidance of a qualified instructor, especially if you are a beginner or have underlying health conditions.

Environment:

Avoid practicing breath-holding in water or in situations where a loss of consciousness could lead to injury.

Listen to Your Body:

Pay attention to warning signs such as dizziness, excessive discomfort, or confusion, and resume normal breathing if they occur.

In conclusion, while breath-holding exercises can offer various benefits, they must be approached with caution. Understanding the underlying physiology and adhering to safety guidelines are crucial to minimize risks and maximize potential advantages.

Skepticism

Q: Gautam, you've spoken about how breathwork transformed your life. But if someone is completely new to breathwork and skeptical about its impact, what would you say to them? How does one truly experience its power?

A: I completely understand skepticism. If you had told me 20 years ago that simply changing the way I breathe could alter my entire life—my mental clarity, my energy levels, my emotional state—I wouldn't have believed you either.

We have been breathing since the moment we were born. It's automatic, effortless, something we take for granted. So the idea that breath can be trained, refined, and consciously used as a tool for transformation might sound strange at first. But here's what I would say to anyone who is skeptical:

Don't believe me. Try it yourself.

Breathwork is not about faith or belief—it's about direct experience. The best way to understand its power is to feel it in your own body. Let me give you a simple example:

Take 20 deep, fast breaths right now, inhaling fully and exhaling quickly.

Now, hold your breath after the last exhale and see how long you can stay without inhaling. Feel what happens in your body—the tingling, the expansion, the shift in awareness. That's energy activation. That's your nervous system waking up. That's the power of breath. Or try this:

Breathe in deeply for 4 seconds, hold for 4 seconds, exhale for 6-8 seconds, and repeat this for two minutes. Notice how your mind calms down, your thoughts slow, and your body starts to relax. That's nervous system regulation. That's stress leaving your body.

These are just tiny glimpses into what breathwork can do. Imagine if you practiced it daily, with the right techniques. What would change in your life? When people ask me, "How does breathwork really work?" I tell them—don't understand it. Experience it.

Do you feel tired all the time? Try breathwork for 7 days, and notice how your energy shifts. Do you struggle with stress and anxiety? Practice 5 minutes of slow breathing before bed, and see how your sleep improves. Do you feel mentally scattered, unable to focus? Train your breath, and watch how your mind becomes razor-sharp.

The results speak for themselves.

Breath is the one thing that is with you from the first moment of life to the last. Learning how to use it properly is not just an option—it's the most fundamental skill for a healthier, stronger, and more conscious life. So, to anyone who is skeptical, I say this: Just take one deep, conscious breath right now. Feel it fully. And then ask yourself—what else have I been missing?

Consistency

Q : Gautam, many people struggle with discipline and consistency in breathwork practices. They start with enthusiasm but lose motivation after a few days. How can one make breathwork a lifelong habit rather than just a temporary practice?

A : This is a fantastic question because the real power of breathwork isn't in doing it once—it's in making it a part of your daily life.

Most people start breathwork feeling excited, but after a few days, they stop. Why? Because they treat it like an activity rather than an integrated lifestyle practice. The key to making breathwork a lifelong habit isn't just about motivation—it's about building a system that makes consistency effortless. Here's how:

1. Understand the Deep WHY Behind Your Practice

The biggest reason people quit is because they don't have a strong reason for doing breathwork. They start because they "heard it's good" but haven't internalized why they personally need it.

Ask yourself:

Do I want more energy?

Do I want to overcome stress or anxiety?

Do I want better sleep?

Do I want to improve my athletic endurance?

Do I want to unlock my full mental and physical potential?

When your "why" is strong, quitting is no longer an option.

2. Stack Breathwork with an Existing Habit -Habit Stacking

One of the easiest ways to make breathwork a habit is to tie it to something you already do daily. This removes the effort of remembering to practice.

Examples:

Do 2 minutes of breathwork before brushing your teeth in the morning.

Practice deep breathing right before drinking your morning tea/coffee.

Do 5 rounds of breathing before starting work or a workout.

Use breath retention before bed to improve sleep.

The key is not to create a new routine, but to attach breathwork to something you already do. 3. Start Small, Stay Consistent, the 2-Minute Rule

A common mistake people make is starting too aggressively. They try to practice for 30 minutes daily, and within a week, they burn out. Instead, start with just 2 minutes a day.

2 minutes in the morning.

2 minutes before bed.

That's it. Once it becomes effortless, you can naturally increase the time. The goal is to become the person who breathes consciously every day. Not the person who starts big and quits.

3. Feel the Immediate Benefits. Make it Rewarding

If a habit doesn't feel rewarding, your brain will not want to continue it. The problem is that people often miss the immediate benefits of breathwork because they focus only on long-term results. Here's what I tell my students:

Right after a 2-minute breathwork session, ask yourself:

Do I feel more awake?

Do I feel calmer?

Do I feel more present?

Did that feel good?

Your brain loves immediate rewards. The more you recognize how good breathwork makes you feel in the moment, the more likely you are to continue it.

4. Make It Personal—Find What Works for You

There are hundreds of breathwork techniques, and not every technique works for every person. Some people love slow, controlled breathing. Others need powerful, energizing breathwork.

If one technique doesn't resonate with you, try another. Breathwork is not a one-size-fits-all practice. Experiment, explore, and find what makes you feel the best.

5. Track Your Progress but in a Simple Way

Many people struggle with consistency because they don't realize how much they're improving. A simple way to stay motivated is to track your breathwork. You can try this. Keep a small journal where you write:

How long you practiced (even if it's just 2 minutes).

How you felt before & after OR use a habit tracker app like Habitica, Streaks, or even just marking a calendar.

Seeing your progress visually creates a sense of achievement and momentum.

6. Integrate Breathwork into Daily Activities. Make It Effortless

Many people think they have to set aside separate time for breathwork, but you can practice it while doing other activities.

Walking? Practice rhythmic nasal breathing.

Working? Try box breathing before an important meeting.

Feeling stressed? Do 3 slow, deep breaths before reacting.

In a traffic jam? Use that time to focus on your breath.

When breathwork becomes part of your everyday life, it stops being a "task" and starts becoming who you are.

7. Join my Community of Breathopreneurs

Humans are social creatures. When we do something with others, we are more likely to stay committed.

Join my breathwork workshops.

Engage with my online breathwork groups.

Being part of a community keeps you accountable and makes the journey more enjoyable.

8. Remove All Friction. Make It Easy to Start

One reason people fail to stay consistent is because they make the habit too complicated. You don't need special equipment—just sit and breathe.

You don't need a perfect setting—just start anywhere.

You don't need a long session—even 2 minutes counts.

The easier you make it to start, the more consistent you'll be.

9. Shift Your Identity—Become "A Person Who Breathes"

This is the biggest secret. The moment you stop saying, "I am trying to do breathwork," and instead say, "I am a person who breathes consciously every day," everything changes. When something becomes part of your identity, you don't need motivation anymore. You just do it because it's who you are. Breathwork is not about doing it perfectly—it's about doing it consistently. If you follow these strategies, breathwork will no longer be something you "try" to do—it will become as natural and essential as breathing itself.

So, just take one conscious breath right now. That's where it begins.

Sexual Health

Q : Gautam, there is a growing conversation around the connection between breathwork and sexual health. How does breathwork influence sexual energy, stamina, and overall well-being in this area?

A : Sexual health is not just about physical ability—it's about energy, awareness, and deep connection with oneself and one's partner. What most people don't realize is that breath is directly linked to sexual energy.

In many ancient traditions—whether it's Tantra, Taoist practices, or yogic teachings—sexual energy is seen as a powerful life force that can either be wasted unconsciously or harnessed for vitality, deeper intimacy, and even spiritual growth.

Breathwork plays a major role in sexual health because breathing patterns directly impact blood circulation, arousal, hormone balance, and emotional connection. Here's how:

1. Breathwork Improves Sexual Stamina & Performance

Many people struggle with premature ejaculation, low endurance, or lack of control during intimacy. One of the main reasons for this is shallow, rapid breathing.

When breath is short and uncontrolled, the nervous system stays in a highly reactive state, leading to quick release and lack of endurance.

Conscious breath control like slow, deep diaphragmatic breathing, allows you to slow down, increase control, and extend pleasure.

Techniques like rhythmic breathwork and retention exercises train the body to handle arousal without immediate release.

Practice Tip:

Try deep, slow breathing (inhale 4 sec, hold 4 sec, exhale 6 sec) during intimacy to extend endurance naturally.

2. Breathwork Enhances Blood Flow & Arousal

Strong sexual performance relies on good blood circulation. Breathwork increases oxygenation and improves blood flow, making arousal and pleasure more intense.

Conscious breath control improves circulation to the pelvic region, enhancing erectile function in men and sensitivity in women. Breath-holding techniques (hypoxia training) can increase nitric oxide production, which expands blood vessels and enhances sexual vitality.

More oxygen = better performance, heightened pleasure, and longer stamina. Practice Tip:

Practice breath retention exercises (inhale deeply, hold for 10 sec, exhale slowly). This builds tolerance and improves circulation.

3. Breathwork Regulates Hormones & Libido

Sexual desire and function are controlled by hormones like testosterone, estrogen, oxytocin, and dopamine.

Stress kills libido. When stress hormones (cortisol) are high, sex drive is low. Breathwork activates the parasympathetic nervous system, reducing stress and allowing natural libido to return.

Deep breathing boosts testosterone in men and balances estrogen levels in women, leading to improved sexual desire and vitality.

Practice Tip:

Do coherent breathing (inhale 5 sec, exhale 5 sec, repeat for 5 minutes) to reset hormones.

4. Breathwork Deepens Emotional & Physical Intimacy

Intimacy is not just physical—it's energetic and emotional. Many people experience disconnect, tension, or anxiety during intimacy. Conscious breathing creates deeper presence, relaxation, and emotional connection between partners.

Practicing synchronized breathing with your partner can create a powerful energetic bond, making intimacy more fulfilling.

Practice Tip:

Before intimacy, sit facing your partner and breathe in sync (inhale together, exhale together). This builds connection and trust.

5. Breathwork Helps Overcome Sexual Anxiety & Shame

Many people struggle with sexual anxiety, shame, or past trauma. This affects confidence, performance, and the ability to fully enjoy intimacy. Breathwork regulates the nervous system, helping to release stored fear, tension, or negative emotions around sexuality.

Dynamic breathwork techniques (like Osho's cathartic breathwork) help clear past trauma and reprogram the mind for confidence and pleasure.

Practice Tip:

Try fast, deep breathing for 1-2 minutes, then relax into slow breathing. This releases stuck emotions and helps in letting go.

6. Breathwork Can Transform Sexual Energy Into Creative & Spiritual Power

In Tantric, Taoist, and Yogic traditions, sexual energy is considered the most powerful life force. It can either be used just for physical pleasure or channeled into creative and spiritual energy.

Advanced breathwork techniques help redirect sexual energy to fuel creativity, mental clarity, and deeper states of meditation. Practicing controlled breath-holding and upward energy movement can lead to full-body orgasms, higher states of consciousness, and increased vitality.

Practice Tip:

During heightened arousal, pause, breathe deeply, and visualize energy moving up your spine (instead of just releasing immediately). This preserves energy and enhances pleasure. Breathwork is the gateway to deeper, more powerful sexual energy. Sexuality is not just about the body—it's about breath, energy, and awareness.

If you:

Want better stamina and control → Train your breath

Want heightened pleasure and deeper intimacy → Sync your breath with your partner Want to feel more confident and powerful → Use breathwork to regulate stress and awaken your energy

When you master your breath, you master your sexual energy. And when you master your sexual energy, you master your vitality, creativity, and overall well-being.

Children

Q : Gautam, should young children be encouraged to practice breathwork? If yes, how can they be introduced to it in a way that is natural, fun, and beneficial for them?

A : Absolutely! Breathwork is not just for adults—it can be a life-changing skill for children as well. However, it is crucial to introduce it in a way that feels natural, playful, and engaging, rather than as a forced practice.

Children are naturally intuitive breathers. Watch a baby breathe—they use their diaphragm fully; their whole belly moves with each breath. But as they grow, stress, school pressure, screen time, and environmental factors make their breathing shallower and more restricted. Teaching them simple, fun, and mindful breathing techniques at an early age can help them:

Stay calm under stress.

Develop better focus and concentration.

Improve emotional regulation.

Enhance lung capacity and immunity.

Sleep better and feel more balanced.

However, the approach must be different from adult breathwork. Children don't respond well to long, structured techniques. They learn best through games, stories, and physical activities.

1. Use Fun, Playful Breathing Games

Instead of saying "Sit and do breathwork," make it a game.

Blowing Bubbles

Give them a bubble wand and tell them to take a deep breath in, then exhale slowly to make the biggest bubble possible. This teaches controlled exhalation in a fun way.

Bumblebee Breath (Humming Breath)

Have them inhale deeply and then hum like a bee on the exhale (Bhramari Pranayama). The vibrations calm the nervous system and reduce anxiety.

Teddy Bear Breathing

Ask the child to lie on their back and place a small stuffed animal on their belly. Tell them to breathe in slowly and watch the teddy bear rise and fall.

This encourages deep belly breathing (diaphragmatic breathing).

Balloon Breath

Have them pretend they are inflating a balloon as they inhale and deflating it slowly as they exhale.

This teaches them how to breathe deeply and fully.

Teach "Superpower" Breathing for Emotional Control

Kids face big emotions—anger, frustration, sadness, anxiety. Breathwork can give them a superpower to manage these feelings.

"Dragon Breath" for Anger

Tell them to imagine they are a dragon.

Take a deep breath in through the nose, then exhale forcefully like a fire-breathing dragon. This helps release frustration and pent-up energy.

"Birthday Candle Breath" for Anxiety

Tell them to pretend they are blowing out candles on a birthday cake.

Take a deep inhale, then blow out each candle one by one with short, slow exhales. This helps slow the heart rate and calm anxiety.

"Feather Breathing" for Focus

Give them a feather and ask them to breathe out gently so the feather floats without falling too fast.

This teaches them breath control and focus.

2. Make It a Fun Group Activity

Kids love to do things together. Encourage breathwork in schools, sports teams, and family settings. Parents and teachers can join in the practice to create a positive association. Practicing together makes it more engaging and creates lifelong healthy habits.

3. Keep It Short and Simple

Unlike adults, kids don't need long sessions. Even 2–5 minutes of mindful breathing a day can make a difference.

Instead of making it "a task," integrate it into their daily routine:

Before bedtime for better sleep.

Before exams or homework for better focus.

After an emotional meltdown to calm down.

Before playing sports to increase stamina.

4. Lead by Example—Parents & Teachers Should Practice Too

Children copy what they see, not what they are told. If they see parents or teachers practicing breathwork, they naturally become curious and want to try it too. Parents can breathe together with kids before bed. Teachers can start morning classes with 1-2 minutes of breathing. This makes breathwork a natural part of life, rather than something "extra" to do. All Kids should be taught Breathwork but in a natural, pressure-freeway. Forcing children into structured breathing exercises can have the opposite effect, making them resistant. Instead, let them explore it in a fun and engaging way.

Younger kids (3-8 years old): Make it playful—breathing games, animal sounds, storytelling. Older kids (9-15 years old): Introduce mindful breathing for focus, sports, and emotional control. Teenagers: Teach advanced breathwork for stress relief, better sleep, and mental clarity.

5. Breathwork is a Life Skill for Kids

Teaching children breathwork early in life is like giving them a toolbox for emotional strength, mental focus, and better health.

If we introduce it in a way that feels natural, fun, and useful, they will carry this skill with them forever. So let's not just teach kids to breathe—let's help them breathe better, live better, and grow into more balanced, aware human beings.

Impact on Kids

Q : How does breathwork suggested by you impact brain development & emotional regulation of a kid?

A : Breathwork is more than just a relaxation technique—it has direct neurological, physiological, and psychological effects on a child's development. Scientific studies show that controlled breathing impacts brain function, emotional stability, and cognitive performance in children.

1. Breathwork Supports Brain Development

Breathwork affects the prefrontal cortex, amygdala, and hippocampus—all essential regions for learning, memory, emotional regulation, and decision-making.

Affects the Prefrontal Cortex (Focus & Decision Making):

Studies show that deep breathing increases oxygen flow to the brain, improving focus, impulse control, and problem-solving abilities. This is particularly beneficial for children with ADHD, as controlled breathing helps them stay present and regulate distractions.

A 2019 review found that breathwork improved executive function skills in children by increasing activity in the prefrontal cortex, which is responsible for attention and self-regulation. (Reference: Diamond & Ling, Annual Review of Psychology, 2019)

Regulates the Amygdala (Emotional Control & Anxiety Reduction):

The amygdala is the brain's "alarm system," responsible for fear, stress, and emotional reactions.

Breathwork activates the parasympathetic nervous system, calming the amygdala and reducing anxiety and emotional outbursts.

This is especially helpful for children who experience anger issues, social anxiety, or panic attacks.

Supports the Hippocampus (Memory & Learning):

Oxygen-rich blood enhances hippocampus function, improving memory retention and cognitive processing. Deep nasal breathing has been shown to improve academic performance in children by helping them retain and process new information more effectively.

2. How Breathwork Helps with Emotional Regulation

Children experience big emotions but don't always have the tools to manage them. Breathwork provides an immediate and effective way to control emotional responses.

Reduces Stress & Anxiety:

Controlled breathing lowers cortisol (the stress hormone), helping children feel calmer.

A study found that students who practiced breathwork for just 5 minutes a day experienced a significant drop in anxiety and stress levels before exams.

(Reference: Harvard Medical School, 2022)

Increases Emotional Awareness:

Slow breathing increases heart rate variability (HRV), making it easier for children to shift from frustration to calmness.

Schools that introduced breathing exercises in classrooms reported a drop in behavioral issues and improved emotional resilience among students.

Teaches Children to Pause Before Reacting:

When a child learns to pause and take a deep breath before reacting, they become better at handling conflicts, disappointments, and social interactions.

3. How Breathwork Enhances Physical Health in Kids

Breathwork increases lung capacity, reducing the risk of respiratory conditions like asthma. It boosts immune function by stimulating the lymphatic system, helping the body fight infections. Controlled breathing improves sleep quality, ensuring children get deep, restorative rest. Best Breathwork Practices for Kids (Backed by Science)

Here are scientifically backed breathing techniques that are fun, engaging, and effective for children:

1. "Belly Balloon Breathing" (Diaphragmatic Breathing)

Purpose: Increases oxygen flow, reduces stress, and promotes deep relaxation. How to Do It:

Have the child lie down and place a small stuffed animal on their belly.

Inhale deeply through the nose, making the belly expand like a balloon.

Exhale slowly, watching the stuffed animal move down.

Repeat for 1-2 minutes.

Scientific Backing: Studies show diaphragmatic breathing activates the vagus nerve, promoting calmness.

(Reference: Frontiers in Psychology, 2018)

2. "Bumblebee Breath" (Bhramari Pranayama)

Purpose: Improves focus, reduces frustration, and calms the nervous system. How to Do It:-

Inhale deeply through the nose.

Exhale while humming like a bee (keeping lips closed).

Scientific Backing: The humming sound stimulates the parasympathetic nervous system, lowering blood pressure and anxiety.

(Reference: Journal of Clinical Psychology, 2020)

3. "5-Finger Breathing" (Mindful Breathing for Focus)

Purpose: Helps children reset their focus and regulate emotions.

How to Do It:

Hold one hand out and trace each finger with the opposite hand while breathing.

Inhale as they move up the finger.

Exhale as they move down.

Repeat until all fingers are traced.

Scientific Backing: This technique activates the prefrontal cortex, helping kids regain attention. (Reference: Cognitive Neuroscience Research, 2021)

4. "Dragon Breath" (For Releasing Anger & Frustration)

Purpose: Helps children release excess energy and frustration.

How to Do It:

Have the child take a deep inhale through the nose.

On the exhale, imagine they are breathing out fire like a dragon.

Encourage them to release any anger into the "fire."

Scientific Backing: This technique lowers stress hormones and helps with emotional release. (Reference: International Journal of Stress Management, 2019)

Every Child should Learn Breathwork. Yes, but in an age-appropriate way.

Young children (3-7 years old): Teach through games and stories (e.g., blowing bubbles, teddy bear breathing).

Older kids (8-12 years old): Teach techniques for focus, sports, and calming anxiety. Teenagers (13+ years old): Introduce advanced breath control for stress relief and emotional stability.

4. Breathwork is a Gift for Life

Teaching children breathwork is like giving them a superpower—a natural tool for calmness, confidence, focus, and emotional strength. It is scientifically proven to enhance brain function, reduce stress, and improve overall well-being. It doesn't require special tools—just awareness

and practice. When learned early, it becomes a lifelong skill that helps children navigate challenges with ease.

So, why wait? Let's teach our children the power of their breath—one mindful inhale at a time.

Precautions

Q : Gautam, what breathwork practices do you recommend for people who are weak, very old, or not in good health? Are there any precautions they should take?

A : Breathwork is for everyone, regardless of age or physical condition. In fact, for people who are elderly, weak, or dealing with health challenges, breathwork can be one of the most gentle yet powerful tools to improve their quality of life. However, the approach has to be adapted to their physical limitations and medical conditions.

The key is slow, mindful, and restorative breathing that supports the body without causing strain. Unlike intense breathwork (like rapid breathing or long breath-holds), gentle techniques help with:

Oxygenating the body and improving lung capacity

Lowering stress and reducing anxiety

Enhancing circulation and heart health

Supporting digestion and immune function

Improving sleep and mental clarity

Best Breathwork Practices for Elderly, Weak, or Unhealthy Individuals:

1. Diaphragmatic Breathing (Belly Breathing) – For Energy & Oxygenation

Why? Weak individuals tend to breathe shallowly, which reduces oxygen supply. Deep belly breathing helps bring in more oxygen without straining the lungs.

How to Do It:

Sit or lie down comfortably.

Place one hand on the chest, the other on the belly.

Inhale deeply through the nose, expanding the belly.

Exhale slowly through the mouth.

Repeat for 2-5 minutes.

Science: Studies show diaphragmatic breathing improves oxygenation and reduces stress in elderly patients.

(Reference: Journal of Gerontology, 2021)

2. Coherent Breathing – For Heart Health & Blood Pressure Control

Why? This technique balances the nervous system, slows the heart rate, and reduces high blood pressure, making it ideal for older adults with cardiovascular issues.

How to Do It:

Breathe in for 5 seconds, then out for 5 seconds (total: 6 breaths per minute). Continue for 5-10 minutes.

Science: Studies show coherent breathing improves heart rate variability (HRV), reduces stress, and enhances autonomic nervous system function in seniors.

(Reference: Frontiers in Aging Neuroscience, 2020)

3. Pursed-Lip Breathing – For Weak Lungs & COPD Patients

This technique reduces breathlessness, especially for people with weak lungs, asthma, or chronic obstructive pulmonary disease (COPD).

How to Do It:

Inhale through the nose for 2 seconds.

Purse your lips (as if whistling) and exhale slowly for 4-6 seconds.

Repeat for 5 minutes or as needed.

Science: Research shows pursed-lip breathing improves lung function and eases shortness of breath in elderly and lung-diseased patients.

(Reference: American Journal of Respiratory Therapy, 2019)

4. Alternate Nostril Breathing (Nadi Shodhana) – For Relaxation & Mental Clarity

Why? As people age, mental fog and stress increase. This technique balances brain activity, sharpens focus, and calms the mind.

How to Do It:

Close the right nostril, inhale through the left nostril.

Close the left nostril, exhale through the right nostril.

Reverse the pattern and continue for 5 minutes.

Science: MRI studies show this practice enhances cognitive function and neural plasticity in older adults.

(Reference: Neuropsychology Journal, 2022)

5. Humming Breath (Bhramari) – For Anxiety & Better Sleep

Why? The gentle vibration of humming stimulates the vagus nerve, helping with relaxation, blood pressure, and sleep.

How to Do It:

Inhale deeply through the nose.

Exhale with a long "hmmm" sound (like a bee).

Repeat for 3-5 minutes.

Science: Research shows humming breath reduces anxiety and improves sleep in seniors with insomnia.

(Reference: Sleep Medicine Journal, 2020)

Special Breathwork for Bedridden or Very Weak Individuals:

For individuals who are extremely weak, bedridden, or recovering from serious illness, even sitting and breathing deeply may feel exhausting. For them:

Focus on nasal breathing → Even just breathing in and out through the nose slowly is beneficial.

Use guided breathwork → If they cannot practice alone, they can listen to guided sessions while resting.

Encourage passive breath observation → Simply observing the breath without changing it helps calm the mind and reduce stress.

Precautions for Elderly & Weak Individuals:

Avoid Intense Breathwork – Rapid breathing (like Wim Hof or holotropic breathwork) may cause dizziness or heart strain in older adults.

Start Slowly – Begin with just 1-2 minutes a day and gradually increase.

Breathe Through the Nose – Nasal breathing filters and warms the air, preventing lung irritation.

If Feeling Dizzy, Stop Immediately – Always listen to the body.

Consult a Doctor if Necessary – People with severe respiratory or heart conditions should check with a doctor before starting breathwork.

Breathwork is a Gentle Healing Tool for All Ages.

Breathwork is one of the simplest and safest ways to improve health, especially for the elderly, weak, or chronically ill. Unlike medications or physical therapies, it has no side effects and can be done anytime, anywhere.

For weak individuals: It restores energy and oxygenation.

For elderly individuals: It supports longevity, brain health, and emotional balance. For people with health issues: It improves lung function, heart health, and sleep.

Even just 5 minutes of mindful breathing a day can make a big difference. Age is not a barrier—everyone can benefit from better breathing. You may find me repeating myself, but it is what it is.

Insights

Q : Gautam, as you said, you are not a medical professional, but your 20 years of research, practice, and teaching have given you deep insights into breathwork. Would you say that your experience allows you to share this knowledge with people effectively?

A : Absolutely. I have always been clear that I am not a doctor or medical professional, but what I do have is two decades of direct experience—practicing, experimenting, observing results, and guiding others through breathwork.

Breathwork is not just theoretical for me; it has been a lifeline, a transformation, and a deep exploration of human potential. Over the years, I have worked with athletes, entrepreneurs, elderly individuals, people with anxiety, those recovering from illness, and even skeptics. I have seen firsthand how breath can heal, energize, and transform lives.

What I share is not a substitute for medical advice, but rather a complementary tool—a way to improve physical, mental, and emotional well-being naturally. Breath is something every person has access to, and when used properly, it can be life-changing.

So yes, my journey—filled with real-world applications, personal breakthroughs, and deep research—has given me knowledge that is worth sharing. And if what I have learned can help even one person breathe better, live

better, and feel better, then I believe it's my responsibility
to share it.

Future

Q : Gautam, where do you see yourself 5 to 10 years down the line?

A : In the next 5 to 10 years, I see myself deepening my journey with breathwork, expanding my teachings globally, and helping more people transform their lives through conscious breathing.

Building a Global Breathwork Community:

I want to create a structured, accessible breathwork system that reaches not just individuals but also schools, athletes, corporate professionals, and medical practitioners.

I envision breathwork becoming a daily practice in people's lives, just like exercise and meditation.

Merging Ancient Wisdom with Modern Science:

I aim to collaborate with researchers, doctors, and neuroscientists to further validate and refine breathwork techniques. I want to contribute to studies that prove how breathwork impacts longevity, mental health, and physical endurance.

Writing Books & Conducting Workshops Worldwide:

I plan to write detailed books on breathwork, sharing both my personal experiences and scientific insights. I see myself leading international breathwork retreats, seminars, and online programs to make breathwork accessible to everyone.

Helping People Heal & Unlock Their Potential:

Whether it's stress relief, mental clarity, athletic performance, or deep emotional healing, I want to see breathwork as a mainstream tool for human well-being.

My goal is to make breathwork a recognized and respected practice worldwide. Ultimately, I see myself as a bridge—connecting people with the power of their own breath, helping them unlock their full energy, focus, and peace. In 10 years, I hope to look back and see millions of people breathing better, living healthier, and thriving because they learned to harness the power of their breath.

Surgery and Pregnancy

Q : What about people with recent surgeries and pregnant women ?

A : Pregnant women can practice gentle breathwork but must avoid intense techniques like breath-holding or rapid breathing. Medical consultation is necessary before starting. People recovering from recent surgery should avoid intense breathwork until cleared by their doctor. Gentle, slow breathing may aid recovery, but in above cases medical advice is compulsory.

Experience in Bengaluru

Q : Gautam, you recently visited Bengaluru, and there is a very beautiful botanical garden there. Did you have any special experience?

A : Yes, my visit to Lalbagh Botanical Garden was far more than just a walk—it felt like stepping into a breathing sanctuary of nature, history, and wisdom.

1. Entering the Garden—A Shift in Energy

The moment I walked in, I felt an instant shift in my breath. It was as if my lungs recognized the place before my mind did. The air was denser, richer—filled with something ancient, something alive.

I took a deep breath, and for the first time in a long while, it felt like I wasn't the one breathing—the garden was breathing me.

The morning mist still lingered on the leaves, birds moved lazily across the sky, and soft golden light filtered through the canopy. There was a stillness—not the stillness of emptiness, but the stillness of fullness, of quiet presence.

It was a reminder that nature never rushes, yet everything gets done.

2. The Ancient Trees—The Wisdom Keepers of Time

I was drawn toward the massive old trees, some over 250 years old. Their trunks thick, their roots deep, their branches stretching toward the sky, as if in a silent conversation with the heavens.

Standing next to one, I placed my hand on the rough bark and closed my eyes. I began breathing with the tree, not just next to it.

Inhale—As if drawing wisdom from its roots.

Exhale—Letting go of all unnecessary thoughts.

For a moment, I wasn't just a visitor in the garden—I was part of it.

These trees had stood in the same place through storms, through decades, through the rise and fall of human generations. Yet, they weren't chasing anything. They just existed, deeply rooted, fully present.

It made me think—why do we humans run so much? Always moving, always chasing, always worrying. But here were these trees, doing nothing but being, and yet, they radiated strength, wisdom, and timeless presence.

At that moment, I understood something: Growth doesn't always require movement. Sometimes, deep roots are more important than fast branches.

3. The Glass House—A Moment of Stillness and Energy Expansion

The Glass House, famous for its grand structure and seasonal flower shows, stood like a temple of light in the middle of the garden. I walked inside, found a quiet corner, and just stood there, breathing. A strange thing happened. The longer I stayed still, the more I felt expanded.

It was as if my breath wasn't just moving inside my lungs—it was stretching beyond my body, blending into the air, into the space, into something bigger.

For a few minutes, there was no me, no body—just awareness, just presence. Maybe this is what monks feel in deep meditation. Maybe this is why ancient sages sat under trees. Because at that moment, I felt what I had always searched for—not outside, but within.

4. The Lake—The Breath of Water, The Art of Letting Go

As I walked towards Lalbagh Lake, I noticed the perfect reflection of the trees in the water. I took a breath and observed:

The water didn't hold onto ripples; it let them pass.

The sky changed its colors, but the lake accepted all of them.

There was no resistance, only acceptance.

I closed my eyes and tried something:

Inhale deeply, imagining the vastness of the sky.

Exhale completely, like ripples dissolving in water.

A deep calmness washed over me.

I realized, most of our suffering comes from resisting life. We hold onto disappointments, fears, expectations—when in reality, we are meant to flow, not grip.

Just like the lake reflects without clinging, we are here to experience life without being trapped by it.

5. The Spiritual Experience—Merging with Nature Through Breath

As I sat beneath an ancient tree near the lake, I decided to try something different—silent breath communication with nature.

I took slow, conscious breaths and imagined:

The tree breathing me in, as I breathed it out.

The lake inhaling as I exhaled, and vice versa.

The entire garden moving through my breath.

And suddenly, something shifted.

For a moment, I couldn't feel where my body ended and where the garden began. It was a feeling of complete connection—not just with nature, but with existence itself.

I understood why breath is called 'Prana'—not just air, but life force.

This wasn't a "spiritual" belief—it was a direct, undeniable experience. I wasn't thinking it. I was feeling it.

6. The Final Realization—Breath is the Doorway to Everything

That day, I didn't just walk through a garden—I walked through a living, breathing universe.

The trees whispered the secret of stillness.

The water showed the art of letting go.

The breath revealed the truth of oneness.

And I understood something:

We spend our whole lives searching—for peace, for happiness, for connection. But all we really need to do is breathe, be present, and listen. Because the universe isn't just around us. It is breathing through us. And once you experience that, even for a moment, you can never see life the same way again.

So yes, that visit to Lalbagh Botanical Garden was far more than just a trip. It was a reminder, a lesson, and a gift. A gift that I carry with me in every breath.

Breatharians

Q : Gautam, is it true or possible for humans to get nutrition from breaths? Are there any studies which can tell us something about it? What is your experience?

A : "Yes, there is a concept known as breatharianism, which suggests that the human body can derive sustenance primarily from prana (life force energy) rather than traditional food. Some practitioners claim to have lived for extended periods without solid food, relying on breath, sunlight, and energy absorption techniques.

Scientific research on this is limited and often controversial. While some studies have explored the effects of prolonged fasting, intermittent fasting, and energy absorption, mainstream science has yet to validate the idea that a person can completely survive on breath alone. However, practices like Pranayama, certain yogic techniques, and Qi Gong have demonstrated profound effects on health, energy levels, and even reduced food dependency.

From my personal experience, breathwork has significantly altered my relationship with food. Deep, conscious breathing energizes my body and reduces my need for heavy or frequent meals. While I do consume food, I find that breath practices can sustain my energy levels and improve my overall well-being. I believe that with disciplined practice, a person can rely much more on breath and pranic energy than they ever thought possible."

Life Force

Q : Different cultures, different names for the same life force. Any thoughts?

A : Throughout history, different cultures have recognized a vital life force energy that sustains all living beings. While the names vary, the essence remains the same—this energy is deeply connected to breath and can be harnessed for physical, mental, and spiritual well-being.

1. Prana (India – Yogic Tradition)

In yogic philosophy, Prana is the fundamental life force that permeates everything, including breath, food, and thoughts. It moves through energy channels called nadis and can be controlled through Pranayama (breath regulation). Yogis believe that mastering prana enhances physical health, mental clarity, and spiritual awakening.

2. Qi / Chi (China – Taoist & Traditional Chinese Medicine)

In Chinese traditions, Qi (or Chi) is the vital energy that flows through meridians in the body. Practices like acupuncture, Tai Chi, and Qigong focus on balancing and directing Qi for healing and longevity. Qi is not just breath but also the subtle energy that sustains all life, much like Prana.

3. Lung (Tibet – Buddhist Tradition)

In Tibetan Buddhism, Lung (pronounced "loong") refers to wind-energy circulating within the body. Breathwork and yogic practices like Tummo (Inner Fire) use Lung to generate warmth and energy, even in freezing conditions. Tibetan teachings suggest that controlling Lung influences mental, emotional, and spiritual states.

4. Mana (Hawaii & Polynesian Spirituality)

In Hawaiian and Polynesian traditions, Mana is the spiritual energy or power that exists in people, objects, and nature. The sacred breath (Ha) is believed to cultivate and direct Mana for healing and empowerment. Hawaiian teachings emphasize breath as a way to connect with the universe and strengthen one's inner power.

5. Ruach (Hebrew – Kabbalistic & Biblical Tradition)

In Hebrew, Ruach means "breath," "spirit," or "wind." In Kabbalah and the Bible, Ruach Elohim (Spirit of God) is described as the divine breath that gives life to creation. Breath is seen as sacred, linking humans to the divine and sustaining the soul.

6. Pneuma (Ancient Greece – Stoic & Medical Traditions)

In ancient Greek philosophy, Pneuma means "breath" or "spirit." The Stoics believed that Pneuma was the force animating all living beings and that controlling one's breath led to inner strength and mental clarity. Greek medicine also saw Pneuma as essential for health, circulating as a vital force in the body.

7. Ka (Ancient Egypt – Spiritual & Vital Essence)

In ancient Egypt, Ka was considered the life force that distinguished the living from the dead. Egyptians practiced controlled breathing to align with cosmic energy and sustain the Ka beyond physical life. Breath was believed to be a conduit between earthly existence and the divine.

Despite cultural differences, all these traditions highlight a universal truth: Breath is more than just oxygen—it is a bridge between the body, mind, and soul.

Life force energy (Prana, Qi, Mana, etc.) can be cultivated through conscious breathing, meditation, and movement.

Mastering breathwork can improve health, enhance energy, and deepen spiritual awareness.

Whether through Pranayama, Qigong, or other ancient practices, understanding and harnessing this life force can lead to greater vitality and a deeper connection with existence.

Faiths and Religions

Q : Gautam, are you religious? Are your workshops open to people from all faiths and religions? A : Let me put it this way—I am not extremely religious.

I don't follow any specific religious path, but I respect all traditions because at their core, every faith teaches the same fundamental truth: awareness, presence, and connection with life.

Breath doesn't belong to any religion. It doesn't ask for your name, your background, or your beliefs before entering your lungs. It just flows.

So, my workshops are for everyone—regardless of faith, background, or belief system.

Whether you believe in God, the universe, science, or just good coffee in the morning, breathwork will work for you.

Whether you pray, meditate, chant, or simply sit in silence, breath is a tool that enhances whatever path you follow.

Whether you come from a deeply religious background or consider yourself an atheist, you are welcome.

Breath is the most universal truth we all share. If you are alive, you qualify. No membership required.

Divine

Q : Gautam, over the past one and a half years, you have shared many amazing, divine experiences with me. Do you truly feel that breathwork can enhance one's experience of life and being?

A : Absolutely. But let me begin with a simple, logical question: What is the only thing you have been doing non-stop since the moment you were born?

It's not thinking. It's not speaking. It's not even a feeling.

It's breathing.

Breath is the first action of life and the last thing we do before we leave this world. Everything else—money, relationships, achievements, even identity—comes and goes. But breath remains. And yet, ironically, it is the one thing we give the least attention to.

Now, let's break it down logically:

1. Breath is the Bridge Between the Body and Mind

Every thought you have, every emotion you feel, and every reaction in your body—all are linked to your breath.

When you are anxious, your breath is shallow and fast.

When you are calm, your breath is slow and deep.

When you are angry, your breath is sharp and erratic.

When you are in deep love, your breath is soft and flowing.

So if your breath is controlling your emotions, then wouldn't it make sense to control your breath first, instead of trying to fight emotions directly?

This is why ancient traditions and modern science both agree: Change your breath, and your state of being changes automatically.

2. Breathwork Doesn't Give You Superpowers, It Reveals What Was Always There

Many people expect breathwork to suddenly make them feel like enlightened beings, as if they will float above the ground after one session. That is not how it works.

What breathwork does is remove the layers that block you from experiencing life fully. It clears the noise, the tension, the overthinking—so that you can simply be.

It won't make you a different person.

It won't give you powers you don't already have.

But it will remove the distractions that stop you from feeling what is already within you.

Imagine a lake full of ripples and waves. You can't see the bottom because the surface is too disturbed. The bottom is always there, but you just can't see it clearly.

Breathwork is like stilling the water.

When the breath becomes conscious, the turbulence settles. And in that stillness, you finally see what was always there.

3. The Real Experience of Life is in Presence, Not in Thoughts

Most people live either in the past (regret, nostalgia) or in the future (anxiety, planning). The present moment is just a blur in between. But when you focus on breath, something profound happens—you become fully present.

Think about the most beautiful moments of your life:

Watching a sunrise that made you speechless.

Holding someone you love after a long time.

Laughing so hard that you forget everything else.

In those moments, you were fully present. Your breath was deep, flowing, effortless. Your mind wasn't racing— it was just there. Breathwork doesn't add anything new to life. It just teaches you how to be present in what already exists. And in that presence, life becomes more vivid, more alive, more real.

4. The Mind Wants Complexity, But the Truth is Simple

There are thousands of self-help books, spiritual techniques, and life philosophies out there, all trying to explain how to live better. But the body already knows. The breath already knows.

Have you noticed how, when you sigh deeply, you feel instant relief? That's the body's way of saying:

"Let go. Breathe. This moment is enough."

We complicate things because the mind enjoys complexity. But the deepest truths are always simple. And breath is the simplest, most direct path back to clarity, peace, and energy.

5. Breath Can Take You to Profound, Almost Divine States—But That's Not the Goal

People often ask me if breathwork can lead to spiritual experiences. The answer is yes. There have been moments where, after a deep breath session, I have felt as if my body disappeared, and only awareness remained.

There have been times when, through breath retention, I have experienced a complete silence inside me, beyond thought and identity.

I have witnessed people break down in tears, not out of sadness, but because breath unlocked something deep within them that they didn't even know was there.

But these experiences are not the goal. They are side effects of deep presence. If you chase them, they will run away. But if you just breathe, be still, and allow life to unfold—they come effortlessly.

6. Life is Happening Now, and Breath is the Key to Experiencing It Fully

Breathwork is not magic. It won't solve every problem in life. It won't make bad days disappear. But what it will do is make you more aware. More present. More alive. And that is where true experience begins.

So, do I feel that breathwork enhances life? No.

Breathwork doesn't enhance life—it reveals it.

Because life was always meant to be experienced this deeply.

Intertwined

Q : Gautam, you have often said that everything on this earth is interwoven—spiritual, physical, mental, experiences, feelings, pros and cons, cause and effect. Can you explain this in your words?

A : Yes, because nothing in this universe exists in isolation. Everything is connected—seen and unseen, cause and effect, action and reaction, breath and consciousness.

We like to separate life into categories:

Physical vs. spiritual

Mind vs. body

Logic vs. emotion

Success vs. failure

But the truth is, they are not separate at all. They are all threads in the same fabric, tightly woven together. You cannot touch one without affecting the others.

1. The Body and the Mind Are Not Two—They Are One

Think of a moment when you were deeply stressed. What happened?

Your breath becomes shallow.

Your muscles become tense.

Your stomach feels tight.

Your thoughts become restless.

Now think of a moment when you felt completely at peace. What happened? Your breath was slow and deep.

Your body was relaxed.

Your thoughts were clear.

It's not that the body affects the mind or the mind affects the body. They are the same system. You change one, the other changes automatically.

This is why breathwork is so powerful. It enters through the body but transforms the mind.

2. The Spiritual and the Physical Are Interwoven

People often ask: "Is breathwork physical or spiritual?" The answer is both.

It is physical because it changes how much oxygen enters your body.

It is mental because it alters your state of mind.

It is spiritual because it brings you into deep awareness, where you feel connected to something beyond yourself.

We are not just bodies. We are not just minds. We are consciousness wrapped in a body, experiencing life through emotions, thoughts, and sensations.

When people say, "I want to be more spiritual," I ask them:

"Do you feel the air when you breathe? Do you notice the sun on your skin? Do you hear the sounds around you?"

That is spirituality. Being fully alive in this moment is the highest spiritual experience there is.

3. Cause and Effect—Every Breath, Thought, and Action Creates a Ripple

Every thought, every word, every action has a consequence. Nothing happens randomly. If you breathe deeply, your body relaxes, your mind calms, your energy improves. If you breathe poorly, your nervous system gets tense, your stress increases, your sleep suffers.

This applies to everything in life:

Eat badly → feel sluggish.

Sleep well → wake up energized.

Think negatively → experience negativity.

Think positively → attract better outcomes.

Life is a series of ripples. What you do now creates the next moment.

So if you want to change your future, start by changing your present. The breath is a good place to begin.

4. Pros and Cons Exist Together—You Cannot Have One Without the Other

Many people try to escape the "negative" in life. But here's the truth:

Light exists because of darkness.

Happiness feels good because sadness exists.

Courage is valuable only because fear is real.

If life was only pleasure, only happiness, only comfort, we wouldn't even notice it. It is the contrast—the rise and fall, the inhale and exhale, the highs and lows—that make life feel rich. When you accept that everything has pros and cons, you stop resisting life. You start flowing with it.

This is why breathwork follows the rhythm of life: inhale, exhale, hold, release. The cycle continues. Just like life.

5. Everything is Interwoven, Just Like Breath

Think of breath. It is simple, yet it connects everything:

It is the bridge between life and death.

It is the link between thought and body.

It is both effort and surrender.

It reminds us that we are not separate from life—we are life itself.

The Art of Living is the Art of Seeing Connection:

The more you observe life, the more you realize—nothing is truly separate. The physical and the spiritual are two sides of the same coin.

The mind and body are threads in the same fabric.

Every action, no matter how small, ripples through existence.

When you truly see this, life stops feeling random. It starts feeling deeply interconnected, meaningful, and alive. And all of it—the pain, the joy, the struggles, the peace—is part of the same breath of existence. So breathe. Be present. Watch how everything is woven together. That is the secret to experiencing life fully.

Catching a Train

Q : Gautam, can you share the incident when you were late for catching a train, and your whole family was waiting at the platform? How did breath awareness save you?

A : Oh, I remember that day vividly! It was one of those moments when life decides to throw everything at you all at once.

We were heading for a family trip, and I, being a little too relaxed, had underestimated the time it would take to reach the station. While my family was already on the platform, calling me frantically, I was stuck in traffic, barely moving.

1. The Chaos Begins

Taxi or auto, nothing was available, clock was ticking, and my mind was racing:

What if I miss the train?

What will my family think?

How could I mess this up?

My breath mirrored my panic—fast, shallow, and erratic. My chest tightened, and I could feel the onset of anxiety creeping in. That's when I realized: This won't help. I need to control my breath if I want to control the situation.

2. The Shift to Breath Awareness

I decided to practice what I preach.

I started inhaling deeply for 4 seconds, holding for 2 seconds, and exhaling slowly for 6 seconds.

Each breath brought clarity.

The panic began to fade, and I felt my body relax.

As my mind calmed, I noticed things I hadn't before—a shortcut through a side road, which I hadn't considered earlier. With clear thinking, I asked the driver to take it, and we started moving faster.

3. The Sprint at the Station

When we finally reached the station, I had only two minutes to make it to the platform. My family was waving frantically from a distance, shouting, "Run!"

Instead of panicking, I used my breath as my guide:

I took rhythmic breaths while running—inhale for 3 steps, exhale for 4 steps. It helped me conserve energy and prevent the "burnout" most people feel when sprinting. Despite carrying a heavy bag, I felt focused and steady. The breath kept me grounded, even in the chaos.

4. Reaching the Train

With seconds to spare, I reached the platform, breath steady, mind calm, and body ready. Just as I jumped in,my family cheered, but I was still focused on my breath— letting it settle me after the adrenaline rush.

Lessons from That Day:

1. Panic never solves anything—breath does. When your mind is racing, your breath can slow it down.

2. Clear thinking comes from calm breathing. Had I stayed in panic mode, I would've missed that shortcut.

3. Breath is a tool for performance. Running with controlled breathing kept me energized and focused, even under pressure.

Now, whenever life feels overwhelming, I remember that day. The breath didn't just save me from missing a train—it saved me from losing control of myself. And that's a skill you can carry anywhere, whether you're catching a train, handling an argument, or facing life's challenges. Your breath is your anchor—it's always there to bring you back to calm, no matter the storm.

Misconception

Q : What is the biggest misconception people have about breathwork?

A : The biggest misconception is that breathwork is just a relaxation technique. Many think it's only about stress relief or deep breathing exercises. In reality, breathwork is a transformational tool—it influences mind, body, emotions, energy, and even spiritual awareness.

Another misconception is that breathing is automatic, so why train it? Yes, breathing happens on its own, but how you breathe affects everything—from your nervous system to your mental state. A well-trained breath can give you more energy, focus, clarity, and control over emotions.

Meditations

Q : Can breathwork replace meditation? Or are they different?

A : Breathwork and meditation are complementary but different.

Breathwork is active. It uses the breath to alter mental and physical states—whether it's for energy, healing, focus, or emotional release. Meditation is passive. It involves observing thoughts, emotions, and awareness itself without actively controlling them.

For many beginners, breathwork is actually a better way to enter meditation. A restless mind struggles with silent meditation, but breathwork calms the nervous system first—making meditation effortless.

Perfect Way

Q : Is there a perfect way to breathe?

A : There is no one-size-fits-all way to breathe because different situations require different breathing techniques.

For focus → Slow, deep, nasal breathing (coherent breathing).

For energy → Rapid breath techniques like Tummo or Wim Hof.

For stress → Exhale longer than inhale (4-7-8 breathing).

For endurance → Breath retention and CO_2 training.

However, in daily life, the best way to breathe is slow, deep, and through the nose—allowing the diaphragm to fully expand.

Anger Control

Q : Can breathwork help with anger and emotional control?

A: 100%. Breath is directly linked to emotion.

When angry, your breath is fast and shallow.

When calm, your breath is slow and deep.

By controlling the breath, you gain control over emotional reactions.

A simple technique: Inhale deeply for 4 seconds, hold for 4 seconds, exhale for 6-8 seconds. This activates the parasympathetic nervous system, cooling the body and mind. Anger is just energy moving fast. Slowing the breath slows the reaction.

Risks

Q : Can breathwork be dangerous? What are the risks?

A : Yes, if done incorrectly or without proper guidance.

Over-breathing (hyperventilation) $\rightarrow$ Can cause dizziness, loss of CO_2, and even fainting. Holding breath too long $\rightarrow$ Can create oxygen deprivation if not done safely. Intense breathwork with heart conditions $\rightarrow$ Can increase heart rate and blood pressure.

Breathwork should be done with awareness, especially advanced techniques. For most people, gentle, rhythmic breathing is completely safe and beneficial.

Sleep

Q : How does breathwork impact sleep?

A : Breath directly affects sleep quality, deep rest, and recovery.

Poor breathing (mouth breathing, shallow breaths) → leads to restless sleep, snoring, and fatigue. Good breathing (nasal breathing, slow rhythm) → leads to deep, restorative sleep.

A simple pre-sleep breathing exercise relaxes the nervous system and prepares the body for sleep.

Perception

Q : Have you ever had a moment where breathwork completely changed the way you saw life?

A: Absolutely. There was a time when I was caught in endless overthinking—chasing goals, feeling restless, always in survival mode. But during a deep breathwork session, I had a sudden realization: "I don't need to fight life, I just need to breathe with it."

That moment changed everything. Instead of controlling life, I started flowing with it. And the more I let my breath guide me, the more life opened up in unexpected, beautiful ways.

Personal Challenge

Q : What was the hardest personal challenge where breathwork helped you the most?

A: Dealing with emotional pain. We're taught to suppress emotions, distract ourselves, or "stay strong." But breathwork taught me that strength isn't about avoiding pain—it's about breathing through it.

There was a time when I was going through personal loss, and I could feel my body resisting grief. Instead of numbing it, I sat, breathed deeply, and let the breath move through my emotions. It didn't erase the pain, but it helped me process it without getting stuck in suffering.

Doubts

Q : Have you ever doubted breathwork or felt like it wasn't working? What did you do?

A : Of course. I think anyone who practices something deeply goes through phases of doubt. There were times when I thought, "Is this really working, or is it just in my head?"

But I realized something—breathwork is like food. You don't eat once and stay full forever. You don't breathe deeply once and stay calm for life. It's a daily rhythm, not a quick fix. So whenever I doubted it, I simply returned to my breath—not to force results, but to reconnect. And every time, the answer was there.

Intuition

Q : How Does Breathwork Improve Intuition?

A : Breathwork is a powerful tool for enhancing intuition because it connects the body, mind, and higher consciousness. Here's how it works:

1. Calms the Mind & Reduces Mental Noise

Intuition often gets drowned out by overthinking and mental clutter.

Conscious breathing (like Pranayama, Box Breathing, or Sudarshan Kriya) activates the parasympathetic nervous system, reducing stress and bringing mental clarity. A calm mind is more receptive to subtle intuitive insights.

2. Increases Awareness & Presence

Intuition is strongest when we are fully present.

Breath awareness pulls attention away from distractions and anchors it in the present moment. This heightened awareness allows us to pick up on subtle cues and inner guidance.

3. Activates the Third Eye (Ajna Chakra)

Many traditions link deep breathing to the activation of the Ajna Chakra (Third Eye), the center of intuition.

Practices like Anulom Vilom (Alternate Nostril Breathing) and Kapalabhati (Skull-Shining Breath) stimulate this energy center, enhancing inner vision.

4. Strengthens Gut Feelings

The gut and brain are deeply connected through the vagus nerve.

Deep breathing stimulates the vagus nerve, improving the gut-brain connection. A well-regulated nervous system makes it easier to trust gut feelings and instinctive decisions.

5. Enhances Connection with Higher Consciousness

Many spiritual practices use breath as a bridge between the physical and the subtle realms. Prolonged breath-focused meditation can lead to moments of deep knowing or spontaneous insights. Breathwork helps bypass logical reasoning and tap into deeper wisdom.

6. Improves Energy Sensitivity

Breath carries Prana (life force energy), and regular practice makes a person more sensitive to energy shifts in themselves and others. This heightened sensitivity allows intuitive messages to be felt more clearly.

By calming the mind, activating energy centers, and improving bodily awareness, breathwork strengthens intuition. The more we tune into our breath, the more we can access the quiet wisdom within us.

Public Speaking

Q : Gautam, you give lectures and have done public speaking. How do you think breathwork can help in this area?

A : Public speaking is one of the most common fears people have. Even the most experienced speakers feel nervous before stepping onto a stage. But the real challenge isn't just speaking—it's managing the energy, emotions, and presence while speaking.

This is where breathwork becomes a game-changer.

1. Controlling Nervousness & Anxiety Before Speaking

Ever noticed how your breath becomes short and shallow before speaking in front of an audience? That's your sympathetic nervous system (fight-or-flight mode) activating, making you feel jittery, shaky, or even blank-minded.

Solution: Use Exhale-Focused Breathing

Inhale for 4 seconds through the nose.

Exhale for 8 seconds through the mouth.

Do this 3-5 times before stepping onto the stage.

Why?

A longer exhale activates the parasympathetic nervous system, calming the body and reducing heart rate. This makes you feel grounded, steady, and in control. I've done this before some of my biggest speaking engagements, and it completely shifts my state from nervous to focused.

2. Projecting a Strong, Confident Voice

A weak breath = a weak voice.

A strong breath = a voice that commands attention.

Many people speak from their throat, not from their diaphragm, making their voice shaky or unstable.

Solution: Diaphragmatic Breathing Before & During Speaking

Place a hand on your belly.

Inhale deeply so that your belly expands.

Exhale fully, feeling your belly contract.

Do this for 2 minutes before speaking.

Why?

This activates the lower diaphragm, creating a powerful, resonant voice instead of a weak, breathless one. It prevents voice cracking or running out of breath mid-sentence. Great speakers don't just speak—they breathe their words into existence.

3. Eliminating the "Ums" and "Ahs" (Speaking with Clarity)

One of the biggest problems in public speaking is filler words like "um," "ah," "you know." These happen when:

The mind races ahead of the breath.

There's too much mental noise.

Solution: Pause & Breathe Between Sentences

Instead of rushing, pause after key points and take a conscious breath. This gives your brain time to organize thoughts and your audience time to absorb what you just said.

Why?

Pausing creates natural authority—people see you as confident and in control. It stops the urge to fill silence with unnecessary words.

The best speakers don't rush—they let the breath create rhythm and impact.

4. Speaking for Long Periods Without Losing Energy

Ever seen speakers who get out of breath, tired, or struggle to finish their sentences? That's because they aren't breathing efficiently while speaking.

Solution: Controlled Exhalation While Talking

When speaking, exhale slowly and evenly instead of forcing air out.

Imagine you're breathing out words, not pushing them.

Extend your exhale to match the length of your sentences.

Why?

This prevents voice fatigue and breathlessness. It allows you to speak for longer without gasping for air. I use this technique, especially during long lectures, and it helps me maintain vocal strength without strain.

5. Creating a Magnetic Presence with Breath Awareness

Great speakers don't just talk—they command a room. Their presence feels bigger, more alive. Solution: Expand Your Breath, Expand Your Presence

Before stepping on stage, take 3 slow, deep breaths and imagine your breath filling the entire room. Breathe in with the thought, "I belong here." Exhale with "I am speaking with confidence and clarity."

Why?

This shifts your internal energy, making you feel expansive and connected to the audience. Breath creates charisma—you don't just speak, you engage.

6. Recovering from a Mistake or Forgetting Words

Everyone makes mistakes—even the best speakers. The difference? How quickly they recover. Solution: The Reset Breath

If you forget a word or lose your train of thought, pause, take a slow breath, and continue. Instead of panicking, let the breath bring you back.

Why?

This prevents rushed corrections or awkward fumbling. It shows you're calm under pressure. Many times, I've used this when I lost my words mid-sentence. Instead of getting stuck, I breathed, reset, and smoothly continued.

7. Enhancing Audience Connection Through Breath Syncing

A secret of great speakers is syncing their breath with the audience's energy. Solution:

Notice the audience's breathing rhythm—are they tense, relaxed, engaged? Adjust your own breath to match their energy and then gradually slow it down. This unconsciously calms the audience, making them more receptive to your words.

Why?

It creates a deep, invisible connection with the listeners. The audience feels your energy before they even process your words.

8. Handling Q&A Sessions with Confidence

Sometimes, unexpected questions can throw speakers off balance.

Solution: Breathe Before Answering

Instead of rushing to respond, take a small pause, inhale, and exhale before speaking. This gives your mind a moment to organize a clear, thoughtful answer.

Why?

It prevents nervous, unstructured responses. It makes you appear calm, collected, and authoritative. I've used this technique in panel discussions, and it always helps me stay composed—even when answering tough or unexpected questions.

Breathwork is the Hidden Superpower of Public Speaking:

Most people think public speaking is about words, voice, or stage presence. But the real secret? It's all in the breath.

Breathe before you speak, and your words will be steady.

Breathe deeply, and your voice will be powerful.

Breathe consciously, and your presence will be magnetic.

Whether it's a small meeting or a large audience, master your breath, and you master the room. And once you learn this, public speaking no longer feels like a performance— it becomes an effortless, flowing conversation with the world.

Crowded Places

Q : Gautam, if we are in crowded places—functions, railway stations, funerals—where many different energies are mixed, do you use breathwork at that time too? If yes, why?

A : Absolutely. In fact, I rely on breathwork even more in such situations.

Crowded places are not just physically overwhelming—they are energetically intense. Whether it's a wedding, a railway station, a political gathering, or even a funeral, the mix of emotions, thoughts, and vibrations in the space can be draining, chaotic, or even unsettling.

Most people don't realize it, but when you are in a place full of people, you are not just breathing air—you are breathing the energy of that space. This is why after attending large gatherings, some people feel exhausted, anxious, or even emotionally heavy without knowing why. Breathwork helps me stay grounded, protected, and centered.

How Breathwork Helps in Crowded Places:

1. Filtering Out Negative or Overwhelming Energy

Have you ever left a funeral feeling deeply heavy—even if you didn't know the deceased personally?

Have you walked into a wedding but felt strangely drained, even though it was a happy occasion?

This happens because your energy field unconsciously absorbs the emotions around you. What I do: Nasal breathing with an extended exhale.

I inhale through my nose, imagining I'm filtering only what I need.

I exhale longer, releasing any unwanted energy.

This acts like an internal energy filter—keeping what's necessary, letting go of what isn't.

2. Staying Calm in Chaotic Environments (Like Railway Stations or Crowded Streets)

Crowded spaces = fast, erratic breathing from people around you.

If you unconsciously match their breathing pattern, you start feeling restless too. What I do: Slow, rhythmic breathing (5-5 count)

Inhale for 5 seconds, exhale for 5 seconds, maintaining a slow, steady rhythm. This keeps my nervous system calm, no matter how chaotic the surroundings. While everyone else is rushing, I remain centered, focused, and in control.

3. Creating an "Invisible Energy Shield" (For Emotional Protection at Funerals or Heavy Places)

Funerals, hospitals, and places of mourning carry a lot of sadness and grief. While compassion is important, absorbing too much of that energy can leave you emotionally exhausted.

What I do: Breathing with awareness of my energy field.

As I inhale, I imagine my breath strengthening my inner energy.

As I exhale, I create a soft, protective barrier around me.

This isn't about blocking emotions—it's about preventing emotional overload.

4. Synchronizing with the Energy of the Event (For Functions & Gatherings)

Every event has a natural rhythm. Some people bring anxiety and stress, while others bring calm and joy. If you're not aware, you get unconsciously pulled into whatever energy dominates the space.

What I do: Breathing in sync with the environment, but at my own pace.

If I want to feel more connected, I subtly adjust my breath to match the pace of the crowd. If the energy is too overwhelming, I slow my breath down to stay in my own space. This allows me to engage with the environment without getting lost in it.

5. Recovering from Energy Drain After Leaving a Crowded Place

Sometimes, even with breath awareness, certain places leave you feeling drained. Too many people talking at once can feel mentally exhausting.

Too much sadness (like funerals) can feel emotionally heavy.

Too much excitement (like parties or weddings) can overstimulate the nervous system. What I do afterward: Grounding Breathwork

Sit quietly for 2 minutes and take deep, belly breaths.

Exhale longer than inhale to release stored tension.

If possible, step outside in fresh air and breathe deeply, feeling the body reset. This helps me clear any lingering energy and return to my natural state. Breath is the best tool for navigating energy in any space.

Crowded places are filled with diverse energies—some uplifting, some overwhelming. But instead of being at the mercy of the environment, breathwork allows me to regulate how I interact with those energies.

It filters what I absorb.

It keeps me calm in chaos.

It prevents emotional overload.

It helps me stay grounded, present, and in control.

So yes, in every crowded place—whether a joyful celebration, a chaotic railway station, or a deeply emotional funeral—I breathe consciously. Because in a world full of mixed energies, breath is the one thing that always brings me back to myself.

Unexpected Benefit

Q : What's the most unexpected benefit you've experienced from breathwork?

A : My ability to read people's energy. Sounds strange, but breath makes you more sensitive to everything around you. The way someone breathes tells you more about them than their words ever could.

I can now sense when someone is nervous, lying, or holding back emotions—just by observing their breath. It's like learning a secret language of energy that most people ignore.

Back in Time

Q : If you could go back in time and teach your younger self one breathing technique, what would it be? Why?

A : I'd teach myself Coherent Breathing (5-5 rhythm)— inhale for 5 seconds, exhale for 5 seconds. It's the simplest yet most powerful way to bring balance.

Why? Because I spent years pushing too hard, stressing over things I couldn't control. If I had learned this breath earlier, I would have handled challenges with calm focus instead of anxiety.

Why Ignore

Q : If breath is so powerful, why do people ignore it?

A : Because it's too simple. People think transformation has to be complicated—books, rituals, intense practices.

But breath? It's so natural that people take it for granted. They don't realize they've been breathing wrong for years until they consciously practice it. Breathwork is like water—it seems ordinary until you realize it's everything.

Death

Q : Does breathwork help us deal with death, and if so, how?

A : Yes. Death is the final exhale, and how we breathe through life determines how we face that moment.

Many spiritual traditions teach dying consciously through breath. The more we practice breath awareness, the less fear we have of letting go—because we realize that life itself is just a series of inhales and exhales.

Breath doesn't just prepare us for death—it teaches us how to fully live before that final breath.

Subject in Schools

Q : If you could design a "breath-based" school subject for kids, what would it look like? A : I'd call it "The Art of Breathing & Thinking."

Kids would learn how to use breath to stay calm before exams.

They'd practice "Breath & Creativity"—using different breathing patterns to boost imagination. They'd do "Breath & Focus Games" to improve memory and attention.

Most importantly, they'd grow up knowing "Your breath is your superpower." Imagine how different adulthood would be if kids learned this from the start!

Mistakes

Q : What's one breathing mistake most people make daily without realizing it?

A: Mouth breathing. It wrecks energy, weakens the immune system, and messes up sleep.

Most people don't realize the mouth is for eating, the nose is for breathing. If you switch to nasal breathing, your health improves without any extra effort.

Altered State

Q : Have you ever had a 'breath-induced' altered state of mind? What was it like?

A: Yes. Once, during deep breath retention, I entered a state where it felt like my body disappeared, but my awareness expanded.

Time slowed down.

My mind stopped its usual chatter.

I felt connected to everything, but there was no "me"— just pure being.

It's hard to explain, but I now understand why ancient yogis used breath to enter deep spiritual states. It's not imagination—it's an actual shift in awareness.

Mandatory

Q : If you could make one breathwork habit mandatory for the entire world, what would it be?

A : 5-5 Coherent Breathing (inhale 5 sec, exhale 5 sec, repeat for 5 minutes). If everyone did this daily:

Stress levels would drop worldwide.

Decision-making would improve.

Relationships would be healthier.

The world would be a much calmer place.

It's the simplest breath that fixes 90% of modern problems.

Energy Sensing

Q : Earlier you talked about sensing energy. Would you like to elaborate more? I know it's a huge topic and I will have to create another book to talk about it in detail. But for now, please share something for our readers.

A : Breathwork is a powerful tool for sensing and shifting different energies within and around us. It connects our body, mind, and spirit, allowing us to tap into subtle vibrations that influence our emotions, awareness, and even our interactions with the world.

Here's how different energies can be felt and experienced through breathwork, with examples:

1. Activating Energy (Pranic or Vital Energy)

Example: Rapid breathing techniques like Bhastrika (bellows breath) or Wim Hof Method create heat and awaken energy in the body. This can make you feel highly energized, tingly, and more alive, as if you've just had a strong cup of coffee but without the crash.

Sensation: Tingling in fingers, warmth in the spine, heightened alertness, an electric-like vibration throughout the body.

2. Grounding Energy (Earth Energy)

Example: Deep belly breathing (Diaphragmatic Breathing or Ujjayi) helps settle scattered energy, bringing a sense of calm and stability. This is often used in yoga or meditation to cultivate a steady, balanced state.

Sensation: A feeling of being centered, feet firmly rooted on the ground, slow and steady heartbeat, relaxed muscles.

3. Emotional Release Energy

Example: Connected breathing (Holotropic Breathwork or Rebirthing Breathwork) can bring up repressed emotions or deep-seated trauma. Some people experience sudden crying, laughter, or shaking as energy blocks are released.

Sensation: Waves of emotion flowing through the body, spontaneous tears or laughter, deep relief after the session.

4. Expansive Energy (Higher Consciousness)

Example: Rhythmic breathing patterns combined with visualization (Sudarshan Kriya or Alternate Nostril Breathing - Nadi Shodhana) can open up higher states of awareness, creativity, and spiritual insight.

Sensation: A sense of lightness, floating, feeling deeply connected to the universe, profound clarity and insights.

5. Transformative Energy (Kundalini Awakening)

Example: Intense breathwork sessions combined with movement and mantra (Kundalini Breathwork or Breath of Fire) can awaken dormant energy at the base of the spine and move it upward.

Sensation: Sudden bursts of energy, shaking, involuntary body movements, deep spiritual experiences.

6. Healing Energy (Regeneration & Self-Healing)

Example: Slow, controlled breathing (Box Breathing or Resonant Breathing at 5.5 breaths per minute) can trigger the parasympathetic nervous system, promoting healing and deep relaxation.

Sensation: A sense of peace, bodily warmth in injured or tense areas, feeling safe and nurtured. Experiencing Energy Differences

Before Breathwork: You might feel sluggish, anxious, or emotionally blocked. During Breathwork: Sensations like tingling, heat, coldness, vibrations, or even visuals may arise.

After Breathwork: You may feel lighter, clearer, more connected, and deeply transformed.

Each breathwork technique can tap into different energy layers, and consistent practice helps in understanding how breath influences physical, emotional, and spiritual energy.

Non-Judgemental

Q : Gautam, we had a chat about being non-judgmental and how Breathwork helps, the other day. Please do share your insights with us.

A : Ah, yes! That was an insightful discussion. Not being judgmental is a deeply liberating state of mind. The human tendency to judge—ourselves, others, situations—often comes from conditioning, insecurities, and past experiences. But judgment is a double-edged sword; the more we judge, the more we trap ourselves in rigid thought patterns that limit our experiences of life.

Let me break it down into a few key insights:

1. Why Do We Judge?

Survival Mechanism: Our brain evolved to categorize things quickly—safe vs. unsafe, good vs. bad—to make decisions for survival. However, in today's world, this instinct can become an unconscious habit that keeps us disconnected.

Ego Identity: Judgment reinforces our sense of self. If we see someone and immediately think, "I would never do that," we reaffirm our identity. But this also creates separation.

Past Conditioning: Our upbringing, society, and experiences shape our biases. Many judgments are not even our own—they are borrowed.

2. Why Is It Important to Let Go of Judgment?

Judgment is limiting—it creates mental barriers.

It drains energy—negative judgments often lead to stress and emotional heaviness. It blocks true connection— when we judge, we stop listening and understanding. It keeps us in an illusion—we see only what we expect to see, not reality.

Now, here's where breathwork comes in.

3. How Breathwork Helps Release Judgment

Judgment is deeply tied to the nervous system. When we are tense, anxious, or in a state of fight-or-flight, we judge more. But when we breathe deeply, slowly, and consciously, something shifts.

a) Breath Awareness (Witnessing Without Judgment)

Breathwork Technique: Slow, natural breathing while observing thoughts without reacting. Simply watching your breath teaches non-reactivity.

Over time, this translates into daily life: You see a person, situation, or thought without immediately labeling it.

b) Resonant Breathing (Shifting from Reaction to Response)

Technique: Inhale for 5 seconds, exhale for 5 seconds (a balanced breath cycle). This brings coherence to the heart and mind, reducing knee-jerk reactions. The mind slows down, and we see situations with more clarity and less bias.

c) Deep Exhalation (Letting Go of Prejudices)

Technique: Inhale deeply, then exhale with an audible sigh or sound.

This physically releases stored judgments and frustrations.

The body learns to "let go" instead of clinging to a perspective.

d) Alternate Nostril Breathing (Balancing Perspectives)

Technique: Nadi Shodhana (inhale through left nostril, exhale through right; then switch).

It balances both hemispheres of the brain—the logical and emotional.

Helps us step out of black-and-white thinking and see multiple perspectives.

4. Breathwork Experience: A Personal Realization

There was a time when I used to get frustrated with people who didn't take health seriously. I would silently judge them: "Why don't they make an effort?" But during a deep breathwork session, something unexpected happened.

As I exhaled deeply, I suddenly felt their struggles—not in my mind, but in my body. It was as if I could feel the weight they carried—their emotional pain, their limitations. And in that moment, judgment melted into understanding.

That experience transformed the way I look at people. Now, whenever I catch myself judging, I take a deep breath and ask, "What if I don't know their full story?"

5. Practicing Non-Judgment Daily

When you notice a judgmental thought, pause and take a deep breath.

Ask: "Am I reacting from conditioning, or am I truly perceiving?"

Instead of labelling, shift to curiosity: "I wonder why this is happening?"

Use a gentle exhale to release the need to be right.

Breath creates space. Judgment tightens. The more we breathe, the more we open up to the truth—not as our mind wants to see it, but as it truly is.

Eliminating Karmas

Q : Any connection between breath work practice and karmic burden?

A : Breathwork practices are believed to play a significant role in reducing or even eliminating karmic burdens from both this life and past lives. Many ancient spiritual traditions suggest that our actions leave energetic imprints, known as karma, which influence our experiences and circumstances. Through intentional breathing techniques, practitioners aim to cleanse these imprints, leading to inner clarity, emotional release, and spiritual growth.

Yogic Breathwork (Prāṇāyāma)

In the yogic tradition, Prāṇāyāma is a disciplined practice of breath control. The word itself means the regulation of prāṇa (life force). Techniques like pūraka (inhalation), kumbhaka (breath retention), and recaka (exhalation) are designed to balance the body's energy channels, or nadis. Yogis believe that unprocessed emotions and karmic patterns reside in the subtle

body, and by regulating the breath, one can cleanse these blockages. This purification process promotes mental clarity, emotional resilience, and spiritual liberation (moksha). Through regular practice, the burdens of past karma can dissipate, allowing practitioners to live with greater freedom and purpose.

Tonglen in Tibetan Buddhism

Another profound breathwork practice is Tonglen, a form of meditation in Tibetan Buddhism. It involves breathing in the suffering of others and breathing out compassion and healing. This practice encourages practitioners to confront and transform suffering rather than avoid it. By cultivating empathy and selflessness, Tonglen helps dissolve karmic patterns of attachment and aversion. This conscious act of exchanging suffering for compassion is believed to accelerate spiritual growth and diminish negative karmic imprints.

Holotropic Breathwork

Developed by psychiatrist Stanislav Grof, Holotropic Breathwork uses deep, rapid breathing in a controlled setting to induce altered states of consciousness. In this expanded state, practitioners may access suppressed memories, unresolved emotions, or even experiences from past lives. By confronting and integrating these experiences, individuals often achieve profound emotional healing. Many report that releasing these stored traumas alleviates karmic baggage, leading to a sense of liberation and renewal.

Shamanic Breathwork

In various indigenous traditions, breathwork is used as a tool for spiritual cleansing and connection with the higher self. Shamanic Breathwork often involves rhythmic breathing accompanied by drumming or music to enter a trance-like state. Practitioners may encounter symbolic visions, ancestral memories, or insights into their karmic path. By journeying through these inner experiences, they can resolve emotional wounds, break free from harmful patterns, and realign with their soul's purpose.

Scientific and Psychological Perspective

From a modern psychological standpoint, controlled breathwork reduces stress, activates the parasympathetic nervous system, and balances the autonomic nervous system. The deliberate act of focusing on the breath fosters mindfulness, allowing individuals to become aware of unconscious patterns and emotions. This heightened self-awareness is essential for breaking free from destructive behaviors often rooted in past karma.

Conclusion

Whether through the disciplined breath control of Prāṇāyāma, the compassionate exchange of Tonglen, the emotional release of Holotropic Breathwork, or the transformative journeys of

Shamanic practices, breathwork serves as a powerful tool for karmic cleansing. By consciously regulating the breath, practitioners not only purify their mind and body but also unravel the deeper layers of their karmic conditioning. Through this inner work, they move closer to spiritual liberation, free from the burdens of past actions.

Myth

Q : What's one breathing myth you'd love to destroy forever?

A : "Deep breathing means taking big breaths."

False. Deep breathing means efficient breathing. If you take big breaths but exhale too fast, you're still over-breathing. If you breathe in deeply but hold tension, you're not doing it right. Real deep breathing is slow, controlled, and natural—not forceful.

Intense Experience

Q : What's the most intense breathwork experience you've ever had?

A : I once did a full hour of continuous circular breathing (no pause between inhales and exhales).

By the end:

My body felt weightless.

My mind was completely silent. I felt like I was floating in pure space.

It was a complete reset—as if my entire nervous system had been washed clean. Breathwork is not about technique—it's about awareness.

No matter where you are in life, just start noticing your breath. The deeper you go, the more you realize:

Breath isn't just life—it's a doorway to everything.

Fear and Anxiety

Q : How can breathwork help people with fear and anxiety?

A : Anxiety is often just uncontrolled breath patterns and high CO_2 sensitivity. During anxiety attacks → breath becomes rapid, shallow, and uncontrolled. Controlling the breath → sends signals to the brain that there is no danger. A powerful technique: Box breathing (4-4-4-4 pattern)

Inhale for 4 seconds, hold for 4 seconds, exhale for 4 seconds, hold for 4 seconds. This resets the nervous system, creating instant calm.

Pain Management

Q : What is the connection between breath and pain management?

A : Breath is a natural painkiller.

When in pain, we tense up, resist, and breathe shallowly, which makes pain worse. But when you breathe deeply and rhythmically, the brain releases endorphins (natural painkillers).

A proven pain-relief method: Humming breath (Bhramari Pranayama)

Inhale deeply, exhale while humming. The vibrations stimulate the vagus nerve, lowering pain perception Many women use breath control during labor, and athletes use it to handle injuries.

Breathing Tea

Q : You often share profound yet simple breathwork techniques that seamlessly blend into daily life—like being conscious of your breath while sipping tea, which you call, breathing tea or walking with breath awareness. These small yet powerful practices turn routine moments into mindful experiences. Would you like to elaborate on how these techniques enhance awareness and well-being in everyday life?

A : Certainly! Breathwork isn't just about structured practice—it's about integrating awareness into everyday life. Simple techniques like holding the breath while sipping tea or walking with breath consciousness can turn routine activities into mindful experiences.

For example, when I drink tea with a brief breath hold or conscious breathing, I fully immerse myself in the warmth, aroma, and taste. It enhances presence and sharpens the senses. Similarly, walking with breath awareness transforms a regular stroll into a meditative practice, syncing breath with steps to cultivate calmness and clarity.

These small yet powerful practices help anchor us in the present moment, reduce stress, and deepen our connection with breath—not as a separate exercise, but as a way of life.

Productivity

Q : Great! Let's explore a few concerns and shed light on how breathwork enhances productivity rather than disrupting demanding work schedules.

A : Sure Meenaa, I would love to talk about this concern. First of all;

Breathwork Enhances Focus, Not Distracts:

Many people assume breathwork is an additional task, but in reality, it sharpens attention and reduces mental fatigue. Research shows that controlled breathing enhances cognitive function, making it an asset for professionals in high-focus jobs like surgeons, pilots, traders, and researchers.

Simple techniques like coherent breathing (5-6 breaths per minute) have been shown to improve concentration and decision-making under stress.

Box breathing (used by Navy SEALs) is a well-known method to increase alertness and emotional stability in high-pressure environments.

Seamlessly Integrating Breathwork Into Work Life:

The beauty of breath awareness is that it doesn't require extra time—it can be practiced while working. Here's how professionals can integrate it effortlessly:

Before an important meeting or presentation: A few deep belly breaths help settle nerves and improve clarity.

During long working hours: Practicing a few minutes of conscious nasal breathing prevents burnout and boosts oxygen supply to the brain.

Between tasks: A simple 2-minute mindful breathing pause helps transition smoothly from one task to another, preventing mental exhaustion.

Can Breathwork Be Practiced Effortlessly?

Absolutely! Unlike meditation, which often requires dedicated time, breathwork can be woven into daily activities. For example:

Typing on a computer? Sync your breath with keystrokes.

Listening in a meeting? Practice soft, slow nasal breathing.

Drinking coffee? Hold the breath briefly before exhaling for better presence.

Breathwork isn't a distraction—it's an enhancement that makes work smoother, improves efficiency, and keeps the mind sharp without adding extra effort!

Too Self Absorbed

Q : Can we have normal regular relationships if we are too engrossed in breath work? Will our relationships not hamper as we will not be present for them and too self one Absorbed?

A : That's a very insightful question, and it's something many people wonder about when diving deep into breathwork or any spiritual practice.

Does Deep Breathwork Affect Personal Relationships?

On the surface, it may seem that being too engrossed in breathwork might make someone detached or self-absorbed. However, the opposite is true when practiced correctly.

Breathwork Increases Presence, Not Isolation

The deeper we go into breath awareness, the more present we become in relationships. Instead of reacting impulsively, we listen more attentively and respond with clarity and compassion.

Many relationship conflicts arise from stress, overthinking, or emotional triggers—breathwork reduces these reactions and helps us engage in relationships from a calmer, more balanced state.

From Self-Absorption to Self-Awareness

There's a difference between self-absorption (being lost in oneself) and self-awareness (understanding oneself deeply).

Breathwork leads to self-awareness, which makes us more emotionally available, not withdrawn. When we understand ourselves better, we can connect with others more authentically.

Healthy Boundaries, Not Disconnection

Deep breathwork practitioners often develop a sense of inner stability, which helps them maintain healthy emotional boundaries in relationships.

It prevents co-dependency or emotional exhaustion while allowing deeper, more meaningful connections.

Breathwork Can Be Shared

Instead of being a solitary practice, breathwork can be something partners, family, or friends engage in together.

Something as simple as taking deep breaths together during a stressful moment or practicing mindful breathing while walking strengthens bonds.

Rather than creating distance, breathwork helps us show up more fully in relationships—with clarity, patience, and emotional balance. It's not about escaping relationships but about being truly present in them.

Milind Soman

Q : How has running alongside Milind Soman influenced your journey as a Breathopreneur? Given his philosophy on fitness, endurance, and mindful living, what key lessons have you learned from his approach to breath control and running? And a lot of congratulations on the completion of your long run. Please share your experiences.

A : Running has always been a passion for me, but the Last Long Run is more than just a run—it's a test of endurance, discipline, and mental strength. Running alongside Milind Soman, a fitness icon, is incredibly motivating. Every year, this challenge pushes my limits and helps me grow physically and mentally.

2022: I completed the Dharamshala to Dalhousie run, covering a challenging route through the Himalayan terrain. The cold weather and steep climbs made it tough, but it was an unforgettable experience.

2023: I ran from Dar es Salaam to Bagamoyo in Tanzania. Running in East Africa was unique—the climate, the scenic coastal route, and the rich cultural experience made it special.

2024: I completed Porbandar to Dwarka, covering 105 km. Running along the coastal belt of Gujarat was spiritually enriching, as it holds deep historical and mythological significance.

Every run is different, but the satisfaction of completing such distances in two days is always rewarding.

Running with Milind Soman is inspiring. His dedication to fitness, his mindset, and his ability to push boundaries motivate me. He leads by example, showing that age is just a number when it comes to fitness. Running alongside him for three years has been an incredible learning experience.

Participating in the 'Last Long Run' for the past three years has been an extraordinary journey, not just because of the physical challenge but also because of the people I have had the privilege to run with.

Milind Soman and Ankita are truly inspiring and loving individuals. Despite their achievements and fame, they are incredibly down-to-earth and simple. Their passion for fitness and endurance is contagious, and their encouragement has been a huge motivation for me during these long runs.

What makes this experience even more special is Milind's family. His entire family exudes warmth and kindness. His sisters are wonderful, and his mother, whom everyone fondly calls Aai, is truly exceptional. She is a symbol of strength and positivity, proving that age is no barrier to fitness. The love and values that Milind carries clearly reflect the beautiful upbringing he has received.

Running alongside Milind Soman has been transformative for me. His minimalist approach, like barefoot running, emphasizes connecting deeply with one's body and environment. This philosophy resonates with my breathwork practice, highlighting the importance of grounding and presence.

Milind's dedication to holistic fitness, incorporating yoga and breath control, has inspired me to integrate these elements into my routine. His emphasis on mental resilience and viewing running as a meditative practice has deepened my understanding of the mind-body connection.

Collaborating with Milind has enriched my journey as a Breathopreneur, blending physical endurance with mindful breath practices.

Timeline

Q : How long does it take to see the benefits of breathwork?

A: Some benefits are instant, while others build over time.

Within 5 minutes: Immediate relaxation, reduced stress.

Within a week: Better focus, energy, and sleep.

Within a month: Improved lung capacity, emotional stability.

Within 3+ months: Higher endurance, better health, stronger mind-body connection.

The key is consistency. Even 5 minutes daily can bring life-changing results.

When?

Q : If someone wants to start the breathwork, where should they begin?

A : Start simple. Many people make the mistake of overcomplicating breathwork.

Best way to begin: Just observe your breath.

Are you breathing fast or slow?

Are you breathing through the nose or mouth?

Are your inhales and exhales balanced?

Then, try this basic practice daily:

Inhale for 4 seconds, exhale for 6 seconds.

Repeat for 5 minutes in the morning or before bed.

That's it. Start small, stay consistent, and let the breath guide you.

Dr. Joe Dispenza

Q : Let's talk about Joe Dispenza now. Please explain how his books have helped you in your journey as breathopreneur.

A : Dr. Joe Dispenza's work has been transformative for many people exploring breathwork, meditation, and consciousness expansion. His books, such as Breaking the Habit of Being Yourself, Becoming Supernatural, and You Are the Placebo, provide a blend of neuroscience, quantum physics, and ancient wisdom. Here's how his teachings align with and support the journey of a Breathopreneur—someone who integrates breathwork into entrepreneurship, healing, and personal transformation.

Reprogramming the Mind with Breath & Meditation

Dispenza explains how our habitual thoughts create our reality. His meditations, which combine deep breathing, visualization, and emotional energy, help rewire the brain for higher consciousness.

As a Breathopreneur, using his methods allows for greater mental clarity, emotional resilience, and a shift from survival mode (stress) to creation mode (flow state).

The Power of the Pineal Gland Activation (Breath & Energy Work)

One of Dispenza's most powerful breathwork techniques involves focusing breath upward toward the pineal gland (Third Eye Chakra).

This practice aligns with ancient Pranayama techniques like Kundalini awakening, which helps activate deep intuition and energy states.

Breathopreneurs can use this method to increase focus, creativity, and deep states of awareness for business and spiritual growth.

Moving from Beta (Stress) to Gamma (Higher Consciousness)

Dispenza teaches how breath and meditation shift brainwave states:

Beta (stress, overthinking) → Alpha (relaxed focus) → Theta (deep intuition) → Gamma (expanded awareness).

This is crucial for entrepreneurs and healers because it enhances problem-solving, intuition, and innovation.

Breath as the Key to Overcoming the Past

His concept of breaking the habit of being yourself resonates deeply with breathwork.

Conscious breathing shifts old emotional patterns, allowing one to create a new identity beyond past limitations.

Many people feel "stuck" in past experiences, but breathwork helps dissolve those energetic blocks.

Becoming Supernatural – Living Beyond Limits

Dispenza's research on people achieving miraculous healings, heightened intuition, and even physical transformations through breath and meditation is groundbreaking.

Breathopreneurs can use these teachings to elevate personal energy, align with their highest purpose, and tap into limitless potential.

Thich Nhat Hanh

Q : How have Thich Nhat Hanh's books, philosophy, and the calmness of his presence influenced your understanding of breathwork? You often quote him while speaking about breath—what key lessons have you integrated into your practice?

A : Thich Nhat Hanh's teachings have deeply influenced my breathwork practice and overall approach to life. His philosophy of mindful breathing—using the breath as an anchor to the present moment—resonates with everything I do.

One of his most profound lessons is: "Feelings come and go like clouds in a windy sky. Conscious breathing is my anchor." This simple yet powerful insight has helped me understand that no matter what emotions arise, the breath is always there to bring me back to balance.

His emphasis on "peace in every step" has also transformed my daily routine. Whether I am running, guiding a breathwork session, or simply sitting in stillness, I focus on each inhale and exhale as a source of calm and presence.

Beyond breathwork, his wisdom on compassionate living and deep listening has shaped the way I interact with people. Breathing mindfully isn't just about personal well-being; it's about creating space for understanding, healing, and transformation.

Thich Nhat Hanh showed me that breath is not just a function—it's a gateway to peace, awareness, and a deeper connection with life itself.

Experimental

Q : Gautam, which new and experimental breathwork exercises do you practice to enhance growth in life?

A : Breathwork is not just about oxygen exchange—it's about expanding perception, deepening awareness, and experiencing life beyond thought. Over the years, I have experimented with various non-traditional, intuitive breath practices that go beyond structured techniques.

Here are some unique and experimental breathwork exercises I personally practice:

1. Breath as a Gateway to Intuition (Breathing Questions & Waiting for Answers)

Instead of overthinking decisions, I have learned to breathe into questions.

How it works:

When I have a doubt, I don't rush for logical answers.

I take slow, deep breaths and "breathe the question" into my awareness.

I don't force an answer—I just wait and observe.

Usually, within a few minutes or hours, the answer comes—not as a thought, but as a deep knowing.

Why does it work?

The conscious mind is limited, but breathwork taps into subconscious intelligence. Sometimes, the best solutions don't come from thinking—they come from breathing and allowing insights to rise naturally.

2. Breathing the Energy of People & Places (Absorbing or Protecting Through Breath Awareness)

Every person, place, and situation has an energy. I use breathwork to either absorb or shield myself from it.

How it works:

If I am in the presence of a highly energized person, I breathe them in—not their air, but their presence, their energy.

If I am in a chaotic, negative environment, I switch to shielding breath. I imagine each inhale strengthening my inner energy field, making me unaffected by external energies.

Why does it work?

Breath is not just about taking in air—it's about taking in vibrations, emotions, and presence. By breathing consciously, I control what enters my being and what stays out.

3. Staring Breath (Eyes-Wide-Open Awareness)

Most meditation techniques teach closed-eye breathwork. I do the opposite—stare, breathe, and merge with what I see.

How it works:

I pick an object—a tree, a flame, a person, even my own hands.

I breathe deeply while staring at it with soft focus, not blinking too much.

After a while, the object and I feel connected—like there's no separation.

Why does it work?

This expands awareness and perception. You begin to feel things, not just see them. It breaks the illusion that we are separate from what we observe.

4. Breathing into the Unknown (Welcoming Discomfort with the Breath)

Most people resist uncertainty, fear, and the unknown. I practice breathing into it.

How it works:

When I feel discomfort, instead of avoiding it, I breathe deeper into it.

I don't try to push it away—I invite it through breath.

Eventually, it loses its grip over me.

Why does it work?

What we resist stays powerful. What we breathe into dissolves into wisdom. This practice helps me grow faster, move through fear, and trust life.

5. Silent Breath Conversations (Communicating Without Words)

Breath is a language. I practice connecting with people, animals, and even objects through breath—not words.

How it works:

I sit in silence with someone, making eye contact.

Instead of speaking, we breathe in sync, feeling each other's presence.

The more I practice this, the more I realize breath carries unspoken emotions and understanding.

Why does it work?

Words often complicate things. Breath, when shared, creates deeper communication without misunderstanding.

6. Micro-Breathing for Manifestation & Shaping Reality

I use breath to plant intentions in the subconscious mind.

How it works:

I hold an intention in my awareness (not words, but the feeling of already having it).

I take small, controlled micro-breaths, as if breathing the intention into my cells. I exhale any doubt or resistance.

Why does it work?

The subconscious is more powerful than conscious effort. When breath is used to embed an idea into the nervous system, it becomes part of our being.

7. Circular Breath for Dissolving Ego Identity

Every breath is a cycle—a loop of giving and receiving. I use circular breathwork to experience oneness with life.

How it works:

I breathe in and out without any pause between inhales and exhales. Soon, it feels like I am not breathing—the universe is breathing me.

Why does it work?

This dissolves the "I" feeling and creates a sense of merging with existence itself. It's an advanced way to let go of self-consciousness and surrender into flow.

8. Breath is Not Just Air—It's a Tool for Evolution.

These are not traditional breathwork techniques. They are explorations. Experiments. Ways to use breath beyond just survival—into awareness, intuition, and transformation.

Some may sound strange. Some may not make sense until you try them. But that's the beauty of breath—it's alive, adaptable, and always waiting to be explored.

So, next time you breathe, don't just do it automatically—breathe with awareness. See where it takes you. Because in that breath, there is more wisdom than the mind can ever comprehend.

Eckhart Tolle

Q : Who doesn't know Eckhart Tolle? You are very impressed by his work yourself. His lectures, books, and experiences must have helped you in life as a whole and as I understand, your life is your breathwork.

A : Absolutely! Eckhart Tolle's teachings have had a profound impact on my life, and since breathwork is my life, his wisdom has deepened my understanding of presence, awareness, and the mind-body connection.

The Power of Now & Breathwork

Tolle's core teaching revolves around being fully present. In breathwork, the breath is the present moment—it's always happening now. His book The Power of Now reinforced my practice by helping me realize that conscious breathing is a direct gateway to stillness and presence.

Silence & the Space Between Breaths

Tolle talks about the "gap" between thoughts—a silent space where true awareness resides. Similarly, in breathwork, the pause between inhales and exhales is where deep transformation happens. His teachings helped me embrace these moments of stillness, allowing intuition and clarity to arise.

Dissolving the Ego Through Breath

Tolle emphasizes that the ego is fuelled by past and future thinking. Deep, conscious breathing dissolves ego-driven anxiety, bringing me into direct experience rather than mental projections. His insights on detaching from identity and thought patterns have aligned perfectly with breathwork's ability to shift consciousness.

Pain-Body & Emotional Release Through Breath

He speaks about the pain-body, the accumulated emotional pain we carry. Breathwork, especially deep diaphragmatic breathing and pranayama, helps release this stored tension. Tolle's guidance made me more aware of emotional blockages and how breath can cleanse them.

Living Through Presence in Daily Life

Beyond structured practice, Tolle's wisdom has helped me integrate breath awareness into everyday moments— walking, listening, working. His reminder that "Life is now" makes every breath a meditation.

His books and talks have not just shaped my breathwork but my entire way of being. Breath isn't just air—it's awareness, presence, and life itself.

Just survival?

Q : Gautam, do you think breath is just an act of survival, or is it something greater?

A : Breath is survival. But it is also the bridge between the seen and unseen.

It is the only function in the body that happens automatically yet can also be controlled. That alone tells you it is special.

Inhale—you take life in.

Exhale—you let go.

Every breath is a cycle, a rhythm, a dance between being and not-being. And the deeper you explore breath, the more you realize—it is not just air moving in and out.

It is life itself.

Intimacy

Q : Gautam, breathwork is often linked to energy, stamina and vitality. I wonder—can breathwork impact personal experiences in intimacy and relationships?

A : Ah, now that's a bold question—but I believe in honesty, so let's talk about it gracefully, scientifically, and openly.

Breathwork absolutely affects intimacy—not just physically, but emotionally, mentally, and even spiritually.

1. The Physical Aspect: Stamina, Control, and Circulation

Let's start with the obvious. Breath controls oxygen levels, blood flow, and nervous system response, all of which play a direct role in sexual health and performance.

Shallow breathing = low energy, weak circulation, and poor endurance.

Deep, rhythmic breathing = enhanced stamina, better blood flow, and natural control.

Many men struggle with premature ejaculation, lack of endurance, or inconsistency in arousal. The root cause? Erratic breathing patterns and nervous system imbalance.

By practicing slow, controlled breathwork, one can train the body to stay relaxed, maintain control, and extend pleasure naturally. No pills, no external aids—just breath awareness.

A simple technique? During intimacy, focus on long exhales (inhale for 4 seconds, exhale for 8 seconds). This engages the parasympathetic nervous system, slowing down the rush and increasing endurance.

2. The Emotional & Mental Aspect: Presence and Deep Connection

Most people approach intimacy physically, but the real depth comes from mental and emotional synchronization.

Ever noticed that when you're stressed, distracted, or overthinking, intimacy feels distant or mechanical?

And when you're relaxed, present, and in tune with your partner, it feels deeply connected?

That's because intimacy is not just about touch—it's about breath, rhythm, and presence.

One of the most powerful practices is synchronized breathing with your partner. It creates a non-verbal connection that deepens the moment.

A personal example: I once guided a couple in a breathwork workshop where they breathed in sync for 3 minutes before even touching. They later told me that they had never felt that level of connection before—without words, without action, just through breath.

It made me realize—intimacy is not about doing more, but about being fully present.

3. The Hormonal Aspect: Breathwork and Libido

Stress kills libido. When cortisol (the stress hormone) is high, testosterone (for men) and estrogen balance (for women) is affected. The result? Low drive, fatigue, and disinterest. Breathwork reduces cortisol and increases oxytocin, the hormone of connection and bonding. It also balances testosterone and estrogen, leading to a naturally heightened sense of desire.

Some breathing techniques, like Tummo or dynamic breathwork, can boost energy and awaken dormant sexual vitality. It's a natural way to reclaim energy, without artificial stimulants.

4. The Spiritual Aspect: Beyond the Physical

Many ancient practices—Tantra, Taoist breathwork, Kundalini awakening—use breath as a tool for transforming sexual energy into higher awareness.

Breath doesn't just fuel intimacy—it can be used to transmute sexual energy into creativity, focus, and even spiritual awakening.

Ancient traditions call this "Prana" in Yoga or "Qi" in Taoist practices. It's life-force energy, and when used correctly, it can be directed towards:

Creativity

Focus

Emotional depth

Spiritual expansion

This is why people who practice breathwork deeply often find themselves more energetic—not just sexually, but in life as a whole.

5. Addressing the Embarrassment Around This Topic

Many people feel shy, embarrassed, or even insecure talking about this. But why? Sexual health is just as important as mental and physical health.

Breathwork teaches self-awareness—and when you are truly in tune with your body, you understand its rhythms, needs, and signals without shame or guilt.

For men: It's not about performance, it's about relaxed presence.

For women: It's not about expectation, it's about natural flow and energy alignment.

Society has made people hyper-focused on external solutions, but the most powerful tool is already within—breath.

6. Breath is the Secret Ingredient in Intimacy

Breath is not just about keeping the body alive—it's about deepening experience.

It controls:

Stamina – Through breath control and nervous system regulation.

Emotional Connection – Through presence and synchronized breathing.

Energy & Libido – Through hormonal balance and circulation.

Spirituality – Through transmutation of energy beyond the physical.

So yes, breathwork has impacted my personal experiences, and it can change the way anyone approaches intimacy and connection. It's not magic—it's physiology, awareness, and presence.

And the best part? It's free. No pills, no treatments—just breath. Now, tell me, isn't that worth exploring?

Patsy Rodenburg

Q : You have mentioned Patsy Rodenburg in past discussions. Would you tell our readers how her work helped you in breathwork?

A : Rodenburg is a renowned voice coach and expert in performance and communication. Her work focuses on presence—being fully engaged in the moment—which, interestingly, aligns with breathwork principles.

While Presence is not specifically a breathwork book, it deeply explores how breath, body awareness, and energy impact our ability to connect with ourselves and others. Here's how it relates to breathwork:

The Three Circles of Energy (Rodenburg's Model)

Rodenburg describes Three Circles of Presence, which are similar to the circles of consciousness you mentioned:

First Circle: Inward, self-conscious, withdrawn energy. Breath is shallow, and people feel disconnected.

Second Circle: Balanced, present, and engaged. Breath is natural and deep, leading to a strong connection with others.

Third Circle: Overpowering, dominant, or scattered energy. Breath may be forced or aggressive.

Her idea of the Second Circle—being fully present, breathing deeply, and engaging naturally with the world—is exactly what breathwork aims to cultivate.

How This Relates to Breathwork

Rodenburg emphasizes breath awareness as the key to presence. She teaches how proper breathing helps speakers, actors, and leaders remain calm, centered, and expressive.

Her techniques align with breathwork traditions like Pranayama and Qi Gong, which also focus on harnessing energy through breath.

Just like in meditation, she teaches how breath controls emotions and helps people shift from stress (First Circle) or overexertion (Third Circle) into flow state (Second Circle).

Practical Takeaway

Breathwork is not just about relaxation—it's about presence. Whether you're meditating, speaking, or making decisions, conscious breathing anchors you in the now, which is the core of both Rodenburg's teachings and advanced breathwork practices.

Runner

Q : Gautam, you yourself are a marathon runner. Any advice to fellow runners from your experience, particularly in the context of breathwork?

A : Absolutely! Breathwork is one of the most overlooked yet most powerful tools in running. Many runners focus on legs, endurance, and speed, but your breath is what actually fuels your run. If your breathing is inefficient, your stamina, recovery, and performance all suffer.

Over the years, I've experimented with various breathwork techniques during training and marathons, and here's what I've learned:

Nose Breathing vs. Mouth Breathing: Which is Better?

Nose breathing is ideal for endurance. But most runners rely on mouth breathing, which:

Causes quick fatigue due to poor oxygen exchange.

Increases dehydration and energy loss.

Can lead to side stitches and cramps.

What works best:

For slow-to-moderate pace: Nasal breathing (inhale and exhale through the nose). For high-intensity sprints: Inhale through the nose, exhale through the mouth.

Pro Tip: If you train yourself to breathe only through the nose during easy runs, over time, your lung capacity improves, and you can sustain longer runs with less effort.

Rhythmic Breathing for Stamina & Injury Prevention

Your breathing pattern should sync with your running stride. The best breathing rhythm for long runs:

Inhale for 3 steps, exhale for 2 steps (3:2 ratio) → Great for endurance.

Inhale for 2 steps, exhale for 2 steps (2:2 ratio) → Ideal for moderate pace.

Inhale for 2 steps, exhale for 1 step (2:1 ratio) → Helps in sprinting or uphill climbs.

Why?

It prevents overexertion by distributing the workload evenly.

It reduces impact on the same foot, minimizing risk of injuries like shin splints.

Breath Holds for Strength & CO_2 Training

Many runners over-breathe, causing them to expel too much carbon dioxide (CO_2), which actually reduces oxygen efficiency.

Training with CO_2 Tolerance (Breath Holds) improves:

Oxygen efficiency → Helping muscles work longer with less oxygen.

Endurance → Delays muscle fatigue.

Mental toughness → Helps handle discomfort better.

Simple CO_2 Tolerance Training:

Take a normal inhale, exhale fully, then hold your breath while walking or running lightly.

Repeat this in sets, gradually increasing the duration of breath-holds over time.

Best done during warm-ups or on easy runs.

This improves your ability to run longer without gasping for air.

The Power of Box Breathing for Pre-Race Calmness

Many runners experience pre-race anxiety, which leads to shallow breathing and an increased heart rate before even starting.

Best calming breathwork before a race.

Why?

Activates the parasympathetic nervous system, keeping you relaxed.

Keeps the heart rate stable, preventing early exhaustion.

Enhances mental focus and race confidence.

Breathing for Sprinting & High-Intensity Phases

When you sprint or push hard, breath control determines how long you can maintain peak speed.

For short bursts of high intensity:

Inhale through the nose, exhale quickly through the mouth.

Use a 1:1 ratio (inhale for 1 step, exhale for 1 step).

Keep the exhale sharp and forceful to expel CO_2 faster.

This prevents oxygen debt and maintains explosiveness.

Recovery Breathwork After a Long Run

Many runners finish a race and keep breathing erratically, which prolongs recovery time.

Best way to recover faster:

Take deep belly breaths instead of shallow chest breaths.

This signals the body to shift from "fight-or-flight" mode to "rest-and-recover" mode.

This reduces muscle soreness, speeds up recovery, and prevents post-run dizziness.

Breath Awareness for Mental Resilience

Long-distance running is not just a physical game—it's a mental one.

In moments of exhaustion, instead of focusing on pain, focus on breath rhythm. If your mind says, "I can't go on," use breath as an anchor to stay present.

A Great Technique: Mantra Breathing

Inhale: "I am strong"

Exhale: "I am steady"

This simple practice shifts your mental state from struggle to strength.

Run with Breath, Not Against It

Most runners fight their breath—but the secret is to run in harmony with it.

Train with nasal breathing to increase efficiency.

Use rhythmic breathing to prevent injuries and increase endurance.

Practice CO_2 breath-holds to improve stamina.

Use Box Breathing to stay calm before races.

Control exhales during sprinting for explosive power.

Recover with slow exhalations to speed up healing.

If you master your breath, you master your run.

Because in the end, running isn't just about speed—it's about breath, rhythm, and flow. And once you align these,

you don't just run—you glide, you enjoy the experience
immensely.

Conclusion

Q : Gautam, as we conclude this interview, what words of wisdom would you like to leave for your readers?

A : If there's one thing I've learned in this journey, it's this—life is happening in this very breath.

Not in the past you keep thinking about.

Not in the future you keep worrying about.

It is here. Right now. Inhale. Exhale. This moment.

We spend years chasing happiness, searching for meaning, running after goals—without realizing that everything we seek is already within us.

You don't need to fix yourself—you need to remember yourself.

You don't need to control everything—you need to surrender to the rhythm of life.

You don't need more—just breathe fully, live fully, and everything will unfold naturally.

The breath is the simplest, most powerful tool you will ever have. Use it wisely.

And above all, never forget—your breath is your guide, your teacher, your home. Trust it. And trust yourself. Let me say this—if you've made it this far in the book, you're already breathing better!

But jokes aside, here are a few important, slightly humorous, but absolutely true life lessons I want you to take with you:

Don't Take Life Too Seriously—You're Just Borrowing Air.

Life is short, but breath is long. If you mess up today, inhale deeply and try again tomorrow.

Overthinking won't solve problems, but deep breathing might make them feel less dramatic. So, when life throws you into chaos, just remember—oxygen is free, stress is optional.

Your Breath is Smarter Than You Are.

You forget names, keys, and passwords—but has your breath ever forgotten to keep you alive?

Trust it. It knows what it's doing.

The next time you're panicking, let your breath do the thinking. Your brain can catch up later.

Your Mood is Just a Few Breaths Away from Changing.

Angry? Exhale louder than your insults.

Stressed? Breathe slower than your boss's emails.

Nervous? Inhale like you own the place, exhale like you don't care.

If all else fails, just take one deep breath and pretend you have your life together.

Stop Running After Happiness—It's Already in Your Lungs.

People spend years chasing peace, success, and fulfillment. But every deep breath gives you instant peace, energy, and clarity—for free!

So, breathe in confidence, breathe out self-doubt.

And if nothing works, just breathe like a monk and pretend you're enlightened.

Breathwork Won't Solve All Your Problems—But It Will Make You Handle Them Better.

You still have to pay bills, go to work, and deal with annoying people.

But at least now, you can stay calm while doing it.

Deep breaths won't make your problems disappear—but they will stop you from throwing your phone at someone.

Breathe, Live, and Laugh More.

At the end of the day, don't just breathe to survive—breathe to thrive.

Take a deep breath before reacting.

Take another before worrying.

And take one more just because it feels good.

Life is just one inhale and one exhale at a time. Make each one count.

About the Author

Meenaa is a writer, storyteller, and seeker of deeper truths. With a keen ability to translate profound wisdom into engaging, relatable narratives, she brings the journey of Gautam Patel's breathwork to life in this book.

Her writing is more than words—it's an experience. She blends insight, clarity, and a touch of soul to make complex ideas accessible to all. Through this book, she invites readers to not just learn about breathwork, but to feel it, live it, and transform through it.

Meenaa's storytelling bridges science, philosophy, and personal growth, making this book a must-read for anyone ready to explore the power of breath.

With every breath, we grow, we heal, we rise
Breath Lifestyle
Breath Lifestyle
In Breath awareness we learn to accept where we are, but we never settle for it.

Be Curious to Breath
Be Curious to See
Always Find A Unique Way
Breath Lifestyle
Every Conscious Breath Makes You Healthy, Stronger & Peaceful.
Breath Lifestyle

Let Every Breath
Becomes Prayer.
Breath Lifestyle
SEE THE LIFE WITH DIFFERENT ANGLE
BREATH LIFESTYLE

TRAIN YOUR BODY TO DO MORE WITH LESS.
BREATH LIFESTYLE
हम बेहद कीमती है।
क्योंकि हम सांस ले सकते हे,
बोल सकते हे,
सुन सकते है,
हमे खुशी होती हे,
हमे दु:ख होता है।

है ना ये सब कमाल का?
Breath Lifestyle

"MADNESS" PEOPLE
MAY SAY,
BUT AS USUAL MY
MADNESS ABOUT MY
BREATH HAS A
METHOD BEHIND IT.
BREATH LIFESTYLE
SOMETIMES WE THINK WE CAN RELAX ONLY WHEN
WE ARE LYING DOWN,
BUT WE CAN RELAX WHILE SITTING, WALKING OR
RUNNING ALSO!
SEE IF IT IS POSSIBLE TO SIT WITH
NO TENSION IN OUR BODY
BREATH LIFESTYLE
BREATH LIFESTYLE
THERE ARE SO MANY METHODS & PATHWAY
AVAILABLE TO ENABLE OUR HIGHER STATE
BREATH WORK IS UNIQUE IN ALL OF THEM
BREATH LIFESTYLE
IN BEGINNING OUR MIND DON'T LIKE
CONSCIOUS BREATHING,
BECAUSE IT CAN'T THINK TOO MUCH,
BUT ONCE WE GET TASTE OF PRESENT MOMENT
THEN WE CAN'T LEAVE THIS PATH!

BREATH LIFESTYLE
हम सांस को हमेशा बहुत ही ग्रांटेड लेते
जैसे उस पर हमारा कोई ध्यान नहीं
और जब सांस पे ध्यान के बढ़ने की शुरु
होती है
तो बिना वजह आनंद आना शुरू होता
आसपास का सब दिखने लगता है.
हम खूबसूरत दुनिया को जीते हे हमारे नि
तरीके से।
Conscious breathing,
Unstoppable energy
Breath Lifestyle

CONSCIOUS BREATHING IS AN ART
THIS IS 24*7 WORK
इसमें विराम नही हे,
लेकिन
ये ही सच में आराम हे।
BREATH LIFESTYLE
In every breath, we find
love, laughter, and
togetherness.
Breath Lifestyle

With Every Breath, we Cherish The Souls Who Make Life Beautiful.
Breath Lifestyle

In every Breath, we find love, laughter, and togetherness.
Breath Lifestyle